AMERICAN FATHERHOOD

AMERICAN FATHERHOOD

A Cultural History

Lawrence R. Samuel

ROWMAN & LITTLEFIELD
Lanham • Boulder • New York • London

Published by Rowman & Littlefield
A wholly owned subsidiary of
The Rowman & Littlefield Publishing Group, Inc.
4501 Forbes Boulevard, Suite 200, Lanham, Maryland 20706
www.rowman.com

Unit A, Whitacre Mews, 26-34 Stannary Street, London SE11 4AB,
United Kingdom

British Library Cataloguing in Publication Information Available

Library of Congress Cataloging-in-Publication Data
Samuel, Lawrence R., author.
American fatherhood : a cultural history / Lawrence R. Samuel.
pages cm
Includes bibliographical references and index.
ISBN 978-1-4422-4810-6 (cloth : alk. paper) — ISBN 978-1-4422-4811-3
(electronic)
1. Fatherhood—United States—History. 2. Fathers—United States—History.
3. Families—United States—History. I. Title.
HQ535.S255 2016
306.874'2—dc23
2015024844

♾ ™ The paper used in this publication meets the minimum requirements of
American National Standard for Information Sciences Permanence of Paper
for Printed Library Materials, ANSI/NISO Z39.48-1992.

Printed in the United States of America

To Freya

CONTENTS

PREFACE

American Fatherhood is largely the result of my becoming a first-time father at an age when most men are seeing their kids (finally!) leave home. Researching the book would be an excellent way to learn much about the dos and don'ts of fathering, I figured soon after having a child, viewing the writing of a cultural history of the subject as a way to draw upon the wisdom of people much wiser than myself.

My own journey to being a mostly full-time dad reflects the transformation of fatherhood in recent decades and demonstrates how having a child can alter one's personal identity and sense of masculinity. Many of the themes in this book resonate with my (limited) experience of fatherhood, making it worthwhile to add a brief personal dimension to the story. A confirmed bachelor, I had no intention of ever becoming a father, seeing parenting as more of a burden than anything else. Well into my fifties, I cherished my freedom and viewed any kind of long-term commitment and responsibilities as things to avoid at all costs. But a few years after meeting "the one," who was significantly younger than I and was keen on having a baby, the idea of being a father began to seem not entirely terrible. "How many times can one go out to dinner?" I asked myself, with a growing sense that there was something missing in my life. In fact, embarking on something new and different for the third and final act of my life sounded rather appealing, my last chance to be part of something larger than myself. We decided to try to have a baby and within two months my then girlfriend was pregnant. My voyage to fatherhood had begun.

Just as many other dads-to-be have reported, the reality that I would likely soon be a father was simultaneously thrilling and terrifying. I had spent little time with kids and was never especially comfortable around them. I did not even understand why so many adults chose to have children, thinking the latter to be basically short, not very smart people. Learning my child was going to be a girl was a real shock, as the kids in both my immediate and extended family were almost all male, so I rather foolishly just assumed she would be a boy. Given that I was going to be a complete novice, however, I came to like the fact that a girl was on the way, as having a daughter would make parenthood even more of a foreign and, hopefully, interesting experience. I began to study children and their parents wherever I might see them, trying to get some sense of what it would be like to be a dad. Over time, I warmed up to the prospect of joining the paternal club and became increasingly enthused (and anxious) as the big day approached.

My future daughter was less than enamored of leaving her dark, warm place and entering this world, however, even as my girlfriend reached full term, so the doctors decided to pluck her out on the very last day possible. On January 26, 2012, I became a first-time father at age fifty-five, my third act now in play. It takes time for some men to warm up to their babies, but I was in love with my daughter the second I laid eyes on and held her in the OR. She looked like both my mom and dad, for one thing, making our relationship love at first sight, at least for me. She, on the other hand, cried and cried for hours after being taken out of her safe cocoon, not at all happy to be brought to this brightly lit and loud place. We left the hospital in a couple of days, beginning our new life together as a family.

It is difficult now to remember much of anything for the first six months of having my child, nature's way perhaps of protecting new parents from any long-term trauma. I did night feedings as mom initially needed to recover from the delivery and, in a couple of months, return to work as her maternity leave ended. (As a writer, I could sleep when the baby slept.) I do recall bonding with my daughter over this period, however, as little can compare with holding and feeding an infant in the wee hours of the morning while the rest of the world (except other new parents!) sleeps. All the usual things—a smile, a laugh, or simply direct eye contact—worked their neurochemical magic, and I was even more hooked.

Over the next few years, she and I became partners in crime, often engaging in the rough-and-tumble sort of play that makes moms very nervous. It's immensely fun to watch her grow up and develop a real personality, much more so in fact than when she was a baby and could not walk or talk. (A typical guy thing.) I find my daughter genuinely hilarious, and I am continually amazed at her observational skills and how perceptive she is, often more so than I am. Sharing what are for her first-time sensory experiences—seeing her own shadow, smelling rain, tasting chocolate—serve as welcome reminders of the wonders of the natural world. An unprompted, matter-of-fact "I love you, dad" is the highlight of my day, as annoying as that may sound to those who have not experienced such a thing. The reluctant father had morphed into an avid one, enjoying every minute (well, not quite every minute, given the sheer determination of any three-year-old) spent with this precious thing. I may not possess some of the childcare abilities of my now wife, but I am certain I contribute in important, unique ways that will help my daughter grow up to be a confident adult. Guiding her through what is to her a brand-new world has allowed me to see many things with fresh eyes, a wonderful gift. I have no doubt that my own father loved me, but he was a product of his generation; I am far more ready, willing, and able to express my emotions with my child—a good thing, I think, for each of us.

I freely admit my experience as a parent so far reads precisely like the cloying cliché I despised when I was living the high life. While I do not have the energy I used to, being an older dad has allowed me to relish our time together. Bestowing as much love to her as possible is clearly my number one priority, with my career and social life mostly distant, happy memories at this point. The ability to scribble a few lines every day or go out for the occasional beer is actually infinitely more pleasurable now that each has become somewhat of a luxury. I could go out more, but I'd simply rather be with her (and I am too exhausted to do anything after she goes to sleep). Don't get me wrong: I miss the adrenaline rush that comes with making a mark in the world through work, and I definitely miss the parties and mayhem that came with being single. But the love one feels for a child simply outweighs and overpowers everything else in its path—again, likely a trick of nature designed to protect and benefit a completely dependent human being. More than that, the love that comes from and is given to a child is pure and unrequited, unlike any other kind a person can experience (including that to or from a spouse).

It is important to note that this is my own, personal story, and I make no judgments of any kind about how other men (or women, for that matter) choose to live their lives. (Indeed, I was happy as a clam before having a kid.) But it's safe to say that for myself, fatherhood has, without too much exaggeration, turned me into a new person. All my previous passions have faded, overshadowed by the mysterious power this little girl has over me. And just like millions of other new dads, I feel like I am somehow more "complete," a bigger and better person than I used to be. In short, I think of myself as more of a man, whatever that might mean, after being reinvented as a father. The pressures that come with being a parent are sometimes overwhelming, the sacrifices one has to make truly astounding, and the patience required for the whole thing unbelievable, but I would not trade them for anything else in the world. Knowing that my daughter will perhaps read this in a decade or so, whether I'll be around or otherwise, makes me very happy.

INTRODUCTION

American Fatherhood: A Cultural History is, as the title makes clear, a cultural history of fatherhood in the United States. More so than intellectual, social, or public histories, which have their own respective agendas, cultural history focuses on the ways a particular subject has found expression throughout a wide swath of everyday life. Surprisingly, no cultural history of American fatherhood currently exists, making this admittedly ambitious project an important one. Much interest currently revolves around fatherhood in America, as the role of men as parents continually evolves. Gender identity is essentially the foundation of the subject and the book, with the dynamics of family another key component of the story. While this book is obviously about fatherhood, by no means does it intend to diminish the role of mothers as parents. The challenges that mothers have faced and continue to face in the workplace and in their personal lives are many, making this study a complementary one to the substantial body of work dedicated to parenting by women.

More broadly, by tracing the story of fatherhood in the United States over the course of the last half century, *American Fatherhood* reveals key insights that add to our understanding of American culture. The book argues that for most of the twentieth century, fatherhood served as a prime source of "feminization" of and for men, with male parents urged to embrace the values and techniques of motherhood. In recent years, however, fathers have rejected this model in place of one that affirms and even celebrates their maleness. After decades of attempting to adopt the parenting styles of women, in other words, men have finally forged a form of child raising that is truer to their own gender. In short, fatherhood has become a means of asserting, rather than denying or suppressing, masculinity, a counterintuitive argument that hopefully will make a significant contribution to the fields of sociology, gender studies, and American history as well as to popular discourse.

The scope of *American Fatherhood* is broad in terms of content and the amount of ground covered. The book begins in the counterculture years, when a new kind of fatherhood began to emerge, and goes right up to today, when the role of dads is arguably more complex than ever. Because fatherhood and, more generally, parenting, touches on many aspects of society, the sweep of the book is wide from a disciplinary aspect as well. Fatherhood intersects with the legal, political, psychological, and sexual spheres, reason enough for the horizontal or lateral approach of the book. Rather than a straight line, readers will learn, the arc or trajectory of fatherhood has taken many twists and turns, making it an unpredictable and often surprising story. Fatherhood is thus not a fixed concept but a fluid one that has both shaped and reflected the cultural climate of the times. Unquestionably, the story of fatherhood became more complex and complicated over the years, as the demands of modern life contributed to the challenges, responsibilities, and expectations of the American dad.

If there is a single thought to be taken away from a relatively long view of fatherhood in the United States, it is that fathers truly matter. Through the first two centuries of the nation's history, this was not believed to be the case, at least with regard to shaping lives in a real, discernible way. "Father is not a very impressive figure in American life," Leonard Benson plainly put it in his 1968 *Fatherhood: A Sociological Perspective*, thinking that a father's essential purpose was to ensure a stable family system.[1] Until the 1970s, in fact, men's role in family life was consistently underestimated, limited primarily to financial provider, no-nonsense disciplinarian, and occasional playmate. It would take numerous research studies to learn that fathers have a direct impact on the emotional well-being of their kids and contribute in other ways substantially different from mothers. Breaking free from deeply seated gender archetypes—reinforced by "attachment theory," positing that children's parental bond was with the mother—was understandably not an easy process for men. The cult of motherhood was (and remains, to some degree) strongly entrenched in our cultural DNA and acts as a barrier to the full expression of fatherhood. This work is essentially the story of that struggle, detailing how men rose to become nearly full partners as parents over the past half century. Presenting men as collectively oppressed in any respect is admittedly a tricky business, but hopefully there is sufficient evidence in this study to justify such a bold claim.

The flip side to the greater recognition of men as parents is the likely scenarios when they are not present. If men are integral to the emotional and cognitive development of their children, it makes perfect sense that kids will suffer psychically if they are not around. That is precisely the case, with dozens of studies conducted over the past few decades confirming as much. Compounding the problem are the many social ills stemming from absentee fatherhood, ranging from poor performance in school to increased incidence of criminality. Fathers' abandonment of their families is thus something that goes well beyond the individuals involved, affecting all of us in some way as American citizens. "Fatherlessness is the most harmful demographic trend of this generation," warns David Blankenhorn, author of *Fatherless America* and the loudest voice of what he and others believe to be "our most urgent social problem."[2] As a non- or pan-partisan issue, fatherlessness has been the target of many corrective efforts over the years, with little or no progress made. Sadly, it could be said that the problem has become woven into the fabric of the country, indelibly linked to the institutional inequities associated with race and class. It is currently difficult to be optimistic about the crisis of fatherless families, with no real solution on the horizon.

A good percentage of men who have left their families no doubt had poor relationships with their own dads, making the problem a recurrent one across generations. Ironically, perhaps, a fair share of great dads also would describe the experience with their own fathers as negative in some way, most often lacking warmth, love, or simply "quality time." Many fathers take a parental approach that is purposely reactionary to the one to which they are most familiar, a determined effort not to pay whatever trauma they suffered forward. While going back to and repairing the damages of the past is not possible, such fathers conclude, one can do one's best that they are not repeated. These dads are thus using their own upbringing as inspiration but in a reverse sense, on a mission to be a better father than the one they had. Doling out massive quantities of attention and affection to a child is this kind of father's modus operandi, often erring on the side of too much nurturing, if there is such a thing. While perhaps not ideal, fathers' giving excess amounts of love to a little one is certainly a better scenario than passing on a paternal history of apathy, neglect, or abuse.

More "truant" dads might reconsider their decision if they were aware of the value of fatherhood not just to their child but to themselves. Not just kids benefit immensely with involved and engaged dads but adults, research has shown, something that holds true across economic lines. Studies have demonstrated the positive effects of parenting among men, with fathers finding the time spent with their children to be rewarding and fulfilling on many levels. Fathers learn much from children by spending both quality and quantity time with them, as any dad will tell you, their perspective of the world irrevocably altered. As well, much is known about kids' psychological gains when they receive paternal love but not the other way around; new research is showing, however, that fathers do indeed benefit from the emotional bond they share with a child (grounded in oxytocin, the "love hormone").

While there is now a very respectable body of scholarly and popular literature dedicated to fatherhood (the parenting section of bookstores is about as large as current affairs), there are other notable research gaps. Not enough attention has been paid to the relationship dynamics between fathers and their children, for example, and specifically how the former evolve as people through those dynamics. "Fathering," as some refer to more active male parenting, is without doubt symbiotic in nature, a fact that is often overlooked. "The father-child relationship is a two-way process, and children influence their fathers just as fathers alter their children's development," wrote Ross D. Parke in his 1996 book simply titled *Fatherhood*. What researchers have learned is that fatherhood typically serves as a principal vehicle for men to find meaning and purpose in their lives, something work and socializing frequently fall short of doing. "Being a father can change the ways that men think about themselves," Parke continued, believing that for many, fatherhood provides a clear sense of identity.[3] The sheer intensity of caring for another human being surpasses most if not all other experiences in life, as father after father has made clear when asked, explaining in part why men want to become dads in the first place. In short, men have rightfully viewed fatherhood as one of if not the only opportunity to become "complete" people, and as a path toward self-realization and perhaps even enlightenment.

Men's "victory" as fathers, if it can be called that, was not just socially and culturally based but biologically as well. Just as women are "hardwired" to be mothers, men are cognitively "programmed" to be fathers, recent research is showing. Neuroscientists are uncovering the secrets to the "daddy brain," that is, the physiological changes that take place as men become and act as fathers. A different kind of biochemistry and neural activity kicks into place after a man becomes a dad, nature's way of advancing a powerful emotional bond between parent and child. From this scientific perspective, the new kind of fatherhood that emerged in the last quarter of the twentieth century can be seen as consistent with the biological makeup of men. Cultural standards were in a sense suppressing a fuller expression of fatherhood, with men able to follow their nurturing instincts now that it is more socially permissible.

The schizophrenic nature of fatherhood in America—beloved when the dad is actively involved and scorned when he is not—speaks to the complexity of the subject and its many contradictions. On the surface, for example, the decline of patriarchal power over the last century and a half can be seen as a direct threat to men, eroding their social and economic currency. However, the feminization of American culture opened up a window for men to assume a larger domestic role, particularly over the last few decades when women made great strides in the workplace. Women's pursuit of equal rights helped make it possible for fathers to emulate mothers, in other words—a major step for men as parental figures. Later, men would be able to reintegrate masculinity into their parenting model, the second great leap in the history of American fatherhood in the past half century.

While a good thing for everybody—men, women, and children—the transformation of fatherhood was, and to some extent continues to be, a difficult process. Their clearly defined role as family breadwinner and authority figure heavily eroded due to a variety of cultural and social forces, men suffered a kind of collective identity crisis beginning around the nation's bicentennial. For many men, adopting more of a "feminine side" naturally threatened their sense of maleness; the usually steadfast marker of gender had been destabilized. To this day, fatherhood serves as a focal point of ambivalence for men as they attempt to negotiate the rocky terrain of gender identity. Despite all the changes in masculinity since the mid-1970s, male identity continues to be heavily steeped in career-related values like success, achievement, and competitiveness, and personal ones centered around independence. It is the outside world where men (and women) can explore such pursuits, making the domestic arena somewhat of a challenge to a traditional interpretation of masculinity. [4]

Likewise, the responsibilities and level of commitment that come with fatherhood are often in opposition to the kinds of freedoms many men had enjoyed, another source of ambivalence for dads. Giving up a big piece of one's self (or perhaps retiring an "old" self for a "new" self) for the betterment of one's family has represented a cornerstone of conflict for men, especially for baby boomers trained in the ethos that they can have it all. Most men come to realize, however, that the sacrifice of some professional achievements and personal freedoms is well worth it, finding themselves "bigger" and better" people through the wonders of fatherhood. Many men report that they became full adults only when they became a parent, the act of having a child basically forcing one to grow up. Fatherhood is deservedly seen as a prime opportunity to evolve as a human being, with the taking on of responsibility for another life the ultimate act that an individual can perform.

Even if men believed they had found their true calling as dads, it did not mean that they were ready to give up on their careers. Many felt, in fact, they could be their best in each area of life, a sentiment that has caused considerable distress over the past two generations. Guilt has proven to be a running theme in fatherhood over the years as men came to the painful conclusion that they could not give 100 percent to two very different pursuits. Women had earlier faced this very dilemma, of course, finding it difficult or impossible to reconcile their newfound career ambitions with motherhood. For both men and women, disappointment and diminished self-worth was the predictable result for setting the bar too high, with many working parents convinced they were not doing a very good job in either arena.

Baby boomers were determined, however, to achieve excellence in both their personal and professional lives. The supermom of the 1970s and early 1980s gave rise to the superdad of the late 1980s and 1990s, as dual-career parents pushed themselves to, and sometimes beyond, their limits. "Superness" was simply an extreme version of the all-out effort many parents made in raising their children. Rejecting the "Mr. Mom" model of parenting, fathers of the early 1990s recognized not just the opportunity but the need to parent differently than mothers. (This expression of fatherhood coincided, not coincidentally, with the "angry white male" crisis of those recessionary years, a means for men to reassert their masculinity.) Within a couple of years, the "baseball dad"— the male equivalent to the "soccer mom"—had been conceived, an icon of hyper-fatherhood.

Admittedly, the heroic status of fathers who were simply doing what was natural and right can be seen as undeserved. Women had mothered for centuries without it being recognized as a superhuman feat, after all, making the media's fascination with what it termed "the new fatherhood" rather over the top. A perverse interest in celebrity dads only further hyped fatherhood in the 1990s and 2000s, and gave the appearance than anyone could have a fabulously successful career and still be a great parent. Representations of seemingly perfect fathering in the media also likely caused some men to wonder if they were fully cut out to be dads. Conceding that one was not fully committed to parenthood was hard to admit to oneself, much less to others. The very notion of imperfect parenthood is one of our few remaining social taboos, I believe, a reflection of the nearly sacred qualities we have assigned to raising children in the twenty-first century.

Alongside overzealous expressions of fatherhood has come the quest for balance. Balance became a mantra of parenting in the late 1980s, as dads and moms realized that attempting to do or have it all was not just stressful but futile. Corporate America has made some strides in accommodating male employees' need for flexibility (just as it had gradually done for women). Many men are reluctant to take companies up on their offer, however, feeling their careers would suffer if they showed anything less than complete devotion to their job. Judging by how frequently the issue is discussed in the media, the idea of balance is perhaps now the dominant theme in fatherhood and parenting in general. Dads are doing more than ever before but still feel like they are not doing enough, a feeling that working moms have known for considerable time. Despite the near obsession with finding balance, many fathers are caught in an endless loop of guilt, anxiety, and stress as they struggle to be the best parents they can be while not giving up on their careers or social life.

Many other obstacles had to be overcome for men to gain greater respect and responsibilities as parents. It is not an exaggeration to say that fathers were discriminated against and treated as second-class citizens within the domestic arena. Men have long been viewed as somehow biologically handicapped as parents, simply unable in both a physical and an emotional sense to be good caregivers to children. (Research has since proven this untrue.) Custody decisions (the determination by a court of who should raise a child or children) in divorce cases were especially stacked in favor of women, with mothers awarded the legal rights to primary care as much as 98 percent of the time. Fathers went to school on the equal rights movements of women, African Americans, gays and lesbians, and the disabled, using the Constitution to change laws and public opinion about their abilities as parents.

Unfortunately, popular culture was working against fathers, with both television shows and movies typically portraying men as less-than-proficient parents. (Think Homer Simpson and *Mr. Mom.*) Science, too, was doing dads no favors, instilling the idea that men were unnecessary as parents since all that was really needed for women to have a child was their sperm. Some eagerly extrapolated from this scientific fact, using it as evidence to support their claim that the number of parents or their gender mattered little for raising an emotionally healthy child. Backed up by mounds of research, another, pro-father camp countered that all families are not created equal, and that there is no substitute for dads. No such attack was ever launched on mothers as caregivers of children, need it be said, another example of men's marginal status as parents.

As men overcame these various obstacles, the very definitions of fatherhood and masculinity changed, each in a positive sense. More specifically, they expanded, taking on different and broader meanings. Fatherhood grew to become something significantly larger and more diverse than it had been in the postwar era as men's parental roles branched off in new directions. And rather than be confined to married, heterosexual males in their twenties, thirties, or forties, fatherhood came to accommodate single, gay, and older men—a radical transformation from a historical sense. Equally important, the full-time or stay-at-home dad was born, this too challenging the long-held belief that a father's primary responsibility was to bring home the family bacon. Much in part to this inflation and diversification of fatherhood, masculinity became a more fluid concept, incorporating alternative characteristics such as nurturance and sensitivity. "Today there is no single predominant road to manhood," wrote Kathleen Gerson in 1994, describing masculinity at the end of the twentieth century as a "no man's land."[5] Again, after initially looking to women for inspiration in the forging of a new kind of gender identity, men were free to readopt traditional expressions of "guyness." Today, both fatherhood and masculinity can be said to be in a good place, a reflection of our more multicultural and pluralistic society that is more tolerant of difference than ever before.

While I give little attention to it in this book, some mention should be made to what is certainly our biggest public celebration of fatherhood: Father's Day. Every third Sunday in June, families pay tribute to dad by giving him the royal treatment, a way of officially acknowledging his many contributions. Taking dad out to dinner, cooking his favorite meal, or making a simple phone call, sending an email, or texting has become a national institution much like Mother's Day is for moms, with the holiday canonized by Hallmark cards and retailers. If dad has passed on, Father's Day is often when family members visit his place of burial or devote some time to remembering him. Schools have adopted the holiday, using it as an opportunity for students to make a handmade card. The media has been especially attuned to Father's Day, routinely dedicating space and time to dad-related issues on or around the day. (Indeed, many of the sources used for this book were published to coincide with Father's Day, taking advantage of readers' predisposition to be already thinking of dear old dad, regretting his absence, or perhaps pondering why things did not turn out as they might have.)

After humble beginnings in the early twentieth century, Father's Day consistently picked up steam to become the popular holiday it is today in the United States. (Dozens of other countries around the world also commemorate the day.) Hallmark began offering Father's Day cards in the 1920s, helping establish it as a feature of American life. By the 1930s, Mother's Day had become highly commercialized, encouraging retailers to promote Father's Day to repeat their success. While Depression-era consumers were not quite ready for another fabricated reason to part with their money, the appreciation of men serving in the

military during World War II helped retailers' cause immensely, leading to the one-billion-dollar-plus boy-toy bonanza it is today. What is
perhaps most interesting about Father's Day is how presidents throughout the twentieth century made efforts to proclaim it as a national
holiday. Presidents Wilson and Coolidge each honored the day, more
likely as a publicity event for themselves than anything else, but were
rebuffed by Congress when they sought to make it an officially observed celebration. After lying dormant for a few decades, LBJ issued
the first presidential proclamation to honor fathers in 1966, but it would
be President Nixon who successfully turned it into a national holiday in
1972. (Nixon just happened to be in the midst of his reelection campaign when the law was passed.)

Given the number and variety of issues in play in this story, it is
difficult to overstate the importance of fatherhood in American history.
The recasting of fatherhood has had a domino effect over the past half
century, altering the trajectory of many other cultural spheres. Beyond
its crossing of paths with key sites of society, fatherhood is directly
connected with family life, especially relationships with partners and
children. The shifting of the tectonic plates of American fatherhood has
had long-term social consequences, arguably equal to those of the wom-
en's or civil rights movements. With no heroes, milestone events, or
media-friendly demonstrations, however, the revolution in American
fatherhood has gone largely ignored. Despite this historical neglect,
men's remarkable evolution as fathers makes itself evident where it
really matters—in the lives of children. A credible case can be made
that, along with motherhood, fatherhood is the heart and soul of everyday life, the central device that propels us forward. Via their investment
in the next generation, dads determine much of what our collective
future will be like, a heavy but thoroughly worthwhile responsibility.

As Robert L. Griswold showed in his masterful *Fatherhood in America*,
the history of fatherhood in the United States from the turn of the
nineteenth century to the mid-twentieth century is a fascinating one.
American fathers' defining role as family earner or breadwinner was
forged with the rise of industrialization, Griswold explained, with mothers viewed as the designated nurturer to children. Fathers increasingly
left their homes to earn money in the new kind of capitalist economy
that was emerging in the early 1800s, bifurcating parental responsibil-

ities in a sharper way than when households produced income through crafts or agriculture. The result of men spending days in offices or factories was predictable; their bond with children was severely fractured, much in part because they no longer passed on knowledge of their trade to the next generation. Sons played and worked alongside their fathers in fields or workshops in the eighteenth century, a practice that encouraged a strong and enduring familial connection. "In short, the occupational tie between father and son was gradually severed," Griswold wrote; men's central identity was now firmly fixed as a "commuting" worker or employee who provided for his family.[6]

Some have challenged this standard narrative of fatherhood in antebellum America, however. In his *Family Men: Middle Class Fatherhood in Industrializing America*, Shawn Johansen used the letters and diaries of some one hundred middle-class fathers to better understand fatherhood between 1800 and the Civil War. Johansen argued that the "separate spheres" between husbands and wives during these years were not as discrete as some scholars have claimed. Men may have gone to work in the morning and returned at night, but that did not preclude having a considerable degree of interaction with their children. (Indeed, many of today's "great dads" keep a similar schedule, and early nineteenth-century men were not distracted by texts while playing with their kids.) Johansen found little evidence of the widely held "decline" of fatherhood in his analysis of the primary materials, concluding that men were not as absent in family life as popularly believed.[7]

Using a similar set of materials, Stephen M. Frank dispelled myths relating to the next generation of American fathers. Victorian patriarchs were quite a bit less stiff and sober than photographs and paintings suggest, Frank put forth in his *Life With Father: Parenthood and Masculinity in the Nineteenth-Century American North*, and were by no means strangers with their little ones. As well, domestic life was not considered a feminizing force by late nineteenth-century middle-class men but rather was consistent with that era's notion of masculinity. "Throughout the [nineteenth] century fatherhood remained a vital component in the social definition of manhood," Frank wrote, with men active participants in child raising. By parsing the writings of real-life fathers from the past, Johansen and Frank helped demonstrate that fatherhood in the United States has been, more or less, a universal experience. Times change and social and economic swings are inevitable, but the joys of being a dad have been and will remain a constant.[8]

Immediately following World War I, there was a sea change in the concept of fatherhood in the United States as modernism swept through society. As Ralph LaRossa discussed in *The Modernization of Fatherhood: A Social and Political History*, modernity ushered in a new kind of role for fathers, one that was significantly more involved in the caregiving process of children. LaRossa made the case that a "culture of daddyhood" arose in the 1920s, a byproduct of the pronounced rationalism and order of the Machine Age. "The period between World War I and World War II witnessed intensified efforts to sanctify men's relationship with their children and thus constituted a time when the social placement of the American father was very much an issue," he wrote, believing that parental roles were "remapped" over the course of these two decades.[9] Griswold agreed that fatherhood was "reinvented" in the 1920s as it became tied to psychological theories and social order. "Fathers provided a different but essential perspective to the development of their children's personalities," family experts argued at the time, a theme that continues to resonate almost a century later.[10]

Evidence of fathers' increased role in family life can clearly be found in popular magazines after World War I. Fatherhood rather suddenly became "the greatest American invention," as *Outlook* magazine put it in 1919, an experience that men should embrace rather than simply tolerate. Prescriptions for how fathers could "succeed" with their sons were widely published (similar information regarding daughters was noticeably lacking), a reflection of the time's emphasis on progress and efficiency. Not just mothers but fathers were assigned the responsibility of "child training," with the latter urged to "get acquainted" with their sons. Fatherhood was now essentially another job for men, with the same kind of effort expected as in one's career. The goal was to be a "hundred percent father," as *Woman's Home Companion* expressed it in 1922, with fatherhood viewed as a serious undertaking that should be pursued with the sort of dedication and skills employed in the business world.

The stock market crash and Great Depression would interrupt the "culture of daddyhood" formed in the twenties, however. With men's principal role as financial provider damaged or threatened by the economic crisis and weak job market, fathers veered away somewhat from their newly established domestic leanings to affirm their masculinity. "More emphasis was given to fathers as masculine caregivers or male role models" in the thirties, according to LaRossa, as men sought ways to demonstrate their virility and manliness.[11] Griswold concurred that American fatherhood had entered a state of "crisis" during the Depression. "For the millions of fathers who lost their jobs, farms, and income because of the Depression, the thirties were a nightmare that destroyed their sense of manhood and personal identity," he wrote, "the patriarchal order based on male breadwinning, fatherly responsibilities, and female economic dependence" severely shaken.[12]

A key way for fathers to demonstrate their maleness in the thirties was to establish a closer attachment with sons. (Completely the opposite was true for daughters, as a more intimate bond with girls could be seen as a too-close-for-comfort brush with femininity.) Through the 1930s, magazines of the decade reveal, men were exhorted to spend time with their sons in order to be good fathers. "Share your boy's hobby," *Parents* magazine suggested in 1931, with fishing an ideal way to become more familiar with the child. "Be a pal," echoed *Rotarian* in 1935, while *American Home* advised fathers to "tell them a story every night." Such efforts were more cosmetic than substantive, however, as self-doubt had clearly infiltrated the paternal setting. By the mid-1930s, tests for men were commonly featured in popular magazines, their aim to determine how good a father the reader was. Wives no doubt used the tests to determine whether their spouses were measuring up, not an especially good recipe for domestic bliss.

With the bombing of Pearl Harbor, fatherhood in America again took another major turn. Just as the war got the country out of its economic crisis, so it rescued fatherhood from its weakened, emasculated status during the Depression. As millions of men enlisted in the armed forces, the sacrifice fathers were making helped immeasurably to restore their public persona. "After the difficulties experienced by so many breadwinners in the 1930s," Griswold observed, "the World War II years not only restored men's breadwinning abilities but reaffirmed fathers' critical role in the health of the republic." The nation's social order was rebalanced as men bravely fought for democracy, with fathers now perceived as being at the very center of the American way of life. Along with this shift came a pivot toward a more conservative set of values, something that would strongly shape the country's social and political climate for decades to come.[13] Ralph LaRossa also understood that the war represented a key juncture in the history of fatherhood, so much so that he followed up his earlier book with *Of War and Men: World War II in the Lives of Fathers and Their Families*. The war was "a social and political tidal wave whose impact on fathers and their families was profound," he wrote, seeing that event as having laid the cultural foundation for the postwar narrative of fatherhood.[14]

Again the changing definition of fatherhood could be detected in popular magazines of the period. Whether stationed in the United States or assigned duty overseas, many fathers were immediately separated from their families and homes for months or years, elevating them to heroic figures in the media. The "far-away father," as *Woman's Home Companion* expressed it, obviously put a strain on family life, particularly because there was a significant risk that dad could be wounded or killed in action. Fatherhood thus took on a special role during the war, imbued with the values of sacrifice and patriotism. "Life without father" according to the *New York Times* in 1944, made Americans all the more committed to winning the war as soon as possible, functioning as a unifying force that strengthened national identity. War bond posters played on fathers' contribution to the military effort, as I wrote in my *Pledging Allegiance: American Identity and the Bond Drive of World War II*, serving as a powerful propagandist device and symbol of traditional masculine identity.[15]

The conspicuous absence of fathers impacted many arenas of everyday life on the home front. Father's Day took on a more serious and sober tone, especially among families whose dads would not be coming home from the war. Fathers who remained at home were asked to "stretch" their parenting skills to the children of neighbors who missed their daddies. (Whether fathers should be drafted was a major issue vigorously debated in Congress.) Interestingly, fathers both away from and at home "discovered" their daughters during the war, a natural response to the greater emotional weight associated with being a parent. Still, sons remained the favored child among fathers, with the eldest male child often given the mighty task of serving as "the man of the house" while dad was away. Much joy was of course expressed when "father comes marching home," as *Parents* riffed in 1945, and the foundation laid for a new, postwar role of the American dad.

As soon as fathers came "marching home," postwar Americans enthusiastically embraced the traditional values of family life. Fathers were a key component of this new kind of domesticity, expected not only to provide for the family but to play an active part in raising children. Fatherhood was "the center of a man's identity," Elaine Tyler May suggested in her *Homeward Bound: American Families in the Cold War Era*, a big part of the domestic "containment" based in the home.[16] The cultural climate of the postwar era, heavily defined by consumption, leisure, and suburbanization, was ideal for middle-class fathers to go well beyond their role as financial provider. "Breadwinning remained critical but experts in the 1950s and early 1960s insisted that fathers imbued with a democratic, permissive, nurturing sensibility could produce well-adjusted offspring capable of resisting the new dangers of the age," stated Griswold, such fears including juvenile delinquency, mental illness, and homosexuality. As well, the priority of private over public life enabled dads to invest more time (and money) in children during these years, with newly constructed houses specifically designed for families the perfect setting for a thriving domestic scene.[17]

That fathers should be active and involved in child raising rather than merely being wage earners is evident in magazines targeted to parents. "Don't let your wife have all the fun," *Parents* told new dads about a year after the war ended, with *Ladies Home Journal* writing a few months later that "men make wonderful mothers." Now, with Americans settling into the comfortable confines of consumer capitalism, dads were being counted on to have what *Good Housekeeping* called "paternal instinct" in bringing up the generation who would become known as baby boomers. The domestication of fathers that had taken root during World War II blossomed in the postwar era as part of the pursuit and celebration of the American way of life. While fathers in the 1920s and 1930s were urged to get acquainted with and be a pal to their sons, the next generation of dads was compelled to take on significantly greater responsibilities in family life. Whether it was occasionally fixing dinner, giving mom a weekend off, or explaining the birds and bees to a son or daughter, fathers were integrally involved with the lives of their children. "Children need the masculine touch," *Today's Health* wrote in 1957, the operative belief being that, to paraphrase the name of a popular television show, father really did know best.

Even if dads often played the fool in that and other TV shows of the era, such as *I Love Lucy, Leave It to Beaver, The Adventures of Ozzie and Harriet, The Danny Thomas Show* (*Make Room for Daddy*), and *The Dick Van Dyke Show*, they were seen as possessing a kind of intelligence and sensitivity that was unprecedented in American history. Given the pressures of conformity of 1950s America, however, some men found the paternal roles assigned to them oppressive and stifling. A variety of resources—schools for fathers-to-be, father's clubs, the ubiquitous Dr. Spock, and, if necessary, the local shrink—were available for dads feeling the stress and anxiety of the keep-up-with-the-Joneses times. *Redbook* felt the need to publish an article called "Why Your Husbands Feel Trapped" in 1962, a good example of the conflict and alienation some fathers were experiencing (a major plot point in the period piece *Mad Men*). Some bemoaned the advent of this new, more "feminized" role of fathers in the United States (it represented nothing less than the "decline and fall" of men, according to *Cosmopolitan* in 1955), but such voices were in the minority. The identity of the American dad had been irrevocably altered, but an equivalent transformation lay ahead.

American Fatherhood tells its story chronologically, beginning in the mid-1960s and going right up to today. The mid-1960s marked a major turning point in fatherhood and American society as a whole, making that period a good place to begin this story. As a cultural history should, this book taps into a wide array of sources steeped in the kinetics of everyday life. Popular magazines and newspapers are used extensively, tapping into the "first draft of history" created by journalists. Scholarly books and articles help frame the story and locate it within what is now a legitimate field of study. Fatherhood has been a central theme in television, books, and parenting books, of course, making those sources also worth examining. In terms of scope, this study purposely focuses more on commonalities versus discordances within American fatherhood, while fully acknowledging that inequalities relating to race, class, ethnicity, and sexual orientation exist across those social divisions as they relate to the subject. Likewise, I do not spend much time on teenage or unwed fathers, as such subjects (which deserve their own cultural histories) are diversions from the central thrust of the book. Fatherhood, like any major institution within society, has had its share

of conflict, of course, but it has also served as a unifying force or common denominator that brought people from different backgrounds together. Too many cultural histories are fundamentally divisive in nature, I believe, a byproduct of the current vogue of seeing the past
through the lens of conflict. Collectiveness and shared experiences are
more powerful (and I think more interesting) than the breaking up of
American society into pieces, something more historians might consider
when telling their own stories.

Chapter 1 of *American Fatherhood*, "America's Newest Endangered
Species," tracks fatherhood in the counterculture era. The mid-1960s
through the 1970s were rough years for American fatherhood, I show,
as a host of factors—the hedonistic cultural climate, generational divide, and escalating rates of divorce and deadbeat dads—rocked the
paternal foundation of the country. The postwar model of fatherhood
was in rapid decline, but no new framework had yet formed, leaving
men without a clear sense of how to raise their children. Chapter 2,
"The New Fatherhood," investigates fatherhood in the 1980s, when a
new, more traditional and feminine brand of paternity took hold in the
United States. The media quickly labeled it "The New Fatherhood," a
style of parenting prescribing a high level of involvement on the part of
dads. This decade also gave rise to the "superdad," as the work hard,
play hard ethos of the eighties infiltrated the universe of parenting.
Chapter 3, "The Daddytrack," explores fatherhood in the 1990s, when a
"kinder, gentler" dad emerged. Tens of millions of baby boomers were
determined to get on the "daddytrack" by having a child, making fatherhood, rather suddenly, popular. Best of all, fathers were no longer expected to act like mothers, with men encouraged to reintroduce masculinity into the parenting process.

Chapter 4 of *American Fatherhood*, "The Role of a Lifetime," charts
fatherhood in the first decade of the twenty-first century. Men increasingly described fatherhood as the role (or mission) of a lifetime—a
powerful idea that launched the American dad into a new social orbit.
Fatherhood was an ideal way to find meaning and purpose in life, many
men were concluding, the conduit for a set of emotional experiences
otherwise unavailable. The final chapter, "Manny Knows Best," considers fatherhood over the last few years. Male caregivers ("mannies," a riff
on female "nannies") of children are quite the rage in larger American
cities, a reflection of the new appreciation of and respect for men as

parental figures. Not since before the Industrial Revolution have fathers achieved such a degree of social status, I argue, or been seen as such vital members of the family. The conclusion of the book summarizes key themes and poses questions about the future of this subject in the United States. Will today's masculine father be with us for some time, or will we return to the more feminine model in place for much of the twentieth century? What kind of fathers will the sons of today's "helicopter" parents turn out to be? Should fatherhood and, more generally, American society further Balkanize in the future, will there even be a recognizable narrative of the American dad? These and other questions will be addressed to try to plot the course of American fatherhood in the years and decades ahead.

I

AMERICA'S NEWEST
ENDANGERED SPECIES

In the last generation, the position of the American father has begun
to pale, to fade into the background of our society and our family life.
—C. Christian Beels, 1974

"Where did all these 'hippies' come from?" sociologists and psychologists asked as the counterculture hit full stride during the summer of
1967. Some social scientists had interesting theories about the child-
hoods of these longhaired, not very well-groomed young people who
were becoming increasingly visible in larger urban areas. It was a weak
or absent father, complemented by an assertive mother, that explained
the origins of these apparently aimless youths, a number of experts
suggested. "Hippies are looking for involvement on a group level to
escape the dominant mother," said Richard A. Koenigsberg, who was
teaching a course on hippies at the New School for Social Research in
New York City. Harry Silverstein, a sociologist, also believed that a
functional absence of the father was instrumental in creating the hippie
phenomenon. "He's there, but he didn't take the large, effective role he
could have," he observed, blaming fathers for not being more involved
in the lives of these emotionally lost young people.[1]

While the proliferation of hippies during the Summer of Love was
certainly alarming to many adults, it was hardly the first time experts
cited a lack of paternal influence as a principal cause of perceived
deviant behavior in youth culture. What was new was that much more

disturbing social ills than laziness and hedonism were being acknowledged as triggered by a lack of effectual fatherhood. Studies were showing a clear link between missing fathers and poor school performance, criminal behavior, and pregnancy among adolescents, the beginnings of what would become a major and recurring theme in sociological research. Although there were obviously numerous exceptions, it could be safely said that the social and political turmoil of the counterculture years made a poor backdrop for fathers and older children to establish any kind of connection. The so-called generation gap between fathers and their teenage or young adult children was very real, as a host of issues—Vietnam, consumer capitalism, drugs, and national identity—acted to divide men and their baby boomer offspring.[2]

The counterculture era was equally unsympathetic to the creation of good relationships between fathers and young children. While the postwar model of parenting was clearly breaking down, no new narrative of fatherhood had yet to fill the vacuum, leaving men without any clear sense of how to be an integral part of family life beyond their traditional role as breadwinner. As well, divorce rates were rapidly escalating, and more men were becoming "absentee" fathers by abandoning their children. Even those men who intended to be good fathers after a divorce were routinely denied custody of their children; their role as parent was reduced to part-time play buddy. After bottoming out in the early 1970s, however, fatherhood in the United States began to turn around as it became apparent that men contributed to the development of their children in profound ways that differed from women. By the end of the decade, men were poised to assume a much more significant role in family life, a happy ending to what was a difficult period in the history of American fatherhood.

WHATEVER HAPPENED TO FATHER?

While certain forces of the late 1960s—notably, feminism, the sexual revolution, and a rethinking of the traditional family unit—were clearly working against positive expressions of fatherhood, paternity did benefit from some of the alternative thinking and practices that sprang out of the counterculture. "Naturalness" in all its forms was valued, for example, eliminating much of the shame and embarrassment associated with the human body. Relatedly, more attention was being paid to the physical and emotional aspects of pregnancy, with men increasingly invited into the process. Natural childbirth was becoming popular among more open-minded couples, with mothers-to-be reading books or attending maternity classes offering instruction in breathing techniques during labor. "Expectant" fathers urged their partners to practice these techniques, the beginnings of an ever-increasing level of involvement in their child's birth. Truly innovative hospitals were allowing husbands to be in the delivery room, although the vast majority of men were still directed to waiting rooms while their wives went through labor.[3]

For most men in the late 1960s and early 1970s, the simple fact was that fathering remained a secondary pursuit, subordinate to achieving career-related goals in life or just having a good time. "Fathers sing all the right notes about loving their children," wrote Colman McCarthy in the *Boston Globe* in 1973, "but it is often love at a distance." On a positive note, some men in the public eye were coming to the realization that they were not very good fathers, and were determined to change their ways while there was still time. Joe Garagiola had recently announced he was leaving the *Today* show in order to devote more time to his family, for instance, and Weeb Ewbank, head coach of the New York Jets, was happy to leave the team because he "hadn't had time to be a father to my kids over the years." The comedian Alan King also publicly regretted spending so much time on his career and so little with his sons, something he would change now that one of them was in drug rehab. Some sort of recommitment to parenthood appeared to be in the zeitgeist as the counterculture ran out of steam in the early 1970s, foreshadowing much bigger things soon to come.[4]

In the meantime, however, social critics made note of the feeble state of fatherhood. In his 1974 article for the *New York Times*, "Whatever Happened to Father?," C. Christian Beels keenly charted the decline of the American father over the last generation, putting into words what many sensed but could not express. Beels, a New York City psychiatrist and family therapist, maintained that the fall of the American dad had been more gradual than sudden, this latest dip part of a longer historical process. Patriarchal power in this country peaked in the late nineteenth century, Beels argued, after which came a long slide as women and children gained more prominent positions in society. Not only were they the sole or primary breadwinners for their families, Beels explained, but fathers of the Gilded Age controlled the household spending and, most important, retained final say regarding all aspects of childrearing. Over the next century, a series of movements and events seriously eroded the influence and authority of such men, making the American father a shadow of what he had once been. Women's suffrage around the turn of the century, modernism between the world wars, the cult of domesticity at midcentury, and the recent feminist movement and youth revolution were just the more obvious contributing factors to the waning of the paternal figure. Finally, Western culture's embrace of bureaucracy served as a kind of meta-cause for the tumble of the American father, as large institutions and organizations usurped the autonomy of families and the individual.[5]

Given this framework, it is understandable how sociologists of the late 1960s and early 1970s approached the subject of fatherhood as a problem to solve. Motherhood had been parsed for decades by academics, but very little was actually known about men as parents. This was more reason for scholars and lay people alike to more closely examine fathers' contribution to child raising. Fathers' role as principal breadwinner was assumed and unchallenged even as women made significant strides in the workplace, but perhaps there were other, nonfinancial roles dads played in family life besides fixing the occasional leaky faucet or mowing the lawn. While there was relatively little hard research in fatherhood at this point, there was plenty of anecdotal evidence suggesting that men had a major impact on children that was quite different from that of mothers. "Fathering should be the vital counterpart of mothering," wrote Marjorie R. Leonard in the *New York Times* in 1969, "not simply a biological contribution." Fathers somehow brought out the masculine side of sons and the feminine side of daughters, Leonard, a professor of psychiatry at Albert Einstein College of Medicine, astutely recognized, borrowing on Freudian theory in her analysis.[6]

Going further, Leonard posed some of the consequences when fathers, in her words, "drop out." Sons looked to other role models if their dad was not around, most of them leading the boys down a wayward path. "Boys who reach adolescence without having had sufficient opportunity to identify with their fathers usually have difficulty in deciding who they want to be, where they want to go, and what they want to do with their lives," she observed, anticipating the findings of numerous research studies conducted over the next few decades. For daughters, it was a different but equally problematic issue when fathers opted out of a family. The traditional view that mothers raised girls and fathers raised boys was still very much in currency, but it would be increasingly challenged as more attention was given to dads' relationships with their daughters. Fathers were instrumental in establishing emotional stability and confidence among daughters, especially as related to gender identity and sexuality, early studies in the field were showing, meaning dads had just as much positive influence on girls as boys. "Companionship with father is the young girl's all-important first experience in feeling at ease with the opposite sex," Leonard noted, the absence of which is often a key factor in relationship problems with men down the road.[7]

THIS LITTLE UNDERSTOOD PHENOMENON

Recognizing they had tapped into a largely untouched field located at the intersection of family and gender, sociologists and others in the social sciences dug deeper into the dynamics of fatherhood. The field was arguably born in 1968 with Leonard Benson's *Fatherhood: A Sociological Perspective*, which cited virtually the complete body of literature devoted to the subject published up to that point. David B. Lynn's *The Father: His Role in Child Development* from 1974 did much the same, establishing the boundaries of the field and serving as a jumping off point for sociologists interested in expanding them. Although a good number of articles and books had been written about some aspect of fatherhood, the literature was scattered and lacked empirical support. There was thus ample opportunity to add to what was known about men in paternal roles, especially when compared to the amount of scholarly and governmental material dedicated to motherhood. The United States Census offered all kinds of data about mothers but none on fathers, in fact, with the same kind of partiality toward women exhibited within the new academic arena of gender studies.[8]

Early research into fatherhood was relatively crude yet did often offer interesting insights. One study completed by a team of scholars at Georgetown University in 1970, for example, focused on why men chose to become dads, a very good question. The researchers found, rather expectedly, that different kinds of men made different kinds of fathers, meaning the answer to the question was not a simple one. Some men were first and foremost romantically inclined, finding themselves fathers only because a loving relationship led to pregnancy; others were principally career-minded, but embarked on fatherhood because it just seemed to be the right thing to do; still others were genuinely family-oriented and began thinking in paternal terms soon after getting married. The latter would often find themselves studying children in a playground, mentally preparing themselves for what was to come. If there was any common denominator among all men, it was that fatherhood grew on them immediately after their child came into the world. Being called "Daddy" was often a true milestone, deepening the relationship between father and child. Still, the researchers concluded that most American dads at this time were rather stoic and silent types, more comfortable standing in the shadows of parenthood than in the spotlight.[9]

If American fatherhood as a whole remained a largely undiscovered territory into the 1970s, one can only imagine how the subject of gay dads represented a truly remote region. The sexual revolution and gay liberation movement brought forth a pronounced interest in gay and lesbian studies, but virtually no consideration was paid to homosexual fathers. To many, the very idea of homosexual fathers was oxymoronic, especially in these days before gay men and lesbians were allowed to adopt children. (Homosexuals were "screened out" by both adoption and foster care agencies, and judges routinely denied custody or even visitation rights to fathers believed to be gay.) By the latter part of the decade, however, more academics were beginning to recognize the subculture of gay dads, expanding the parameters of what constituted fatherhood. Scholars at the University of Washington, SUNY Stony Brook, and UCLA all researched some aspect of gay parenting, with much of the work centered around the impact of fathers' or mothers' sexual orientation on their children. In 1978, a landmark article called "Gay Fathers" was published in *Family Coordinator*; the piece served as an exponential leap in scholarly material relating to homosexual dads. In a question-and-answer format, James Walters, editor of the journal and professor of child and family development at the University of Georgia, and Bruce Voeller, co-executive director of the National Gay Task Force, added much to the current understanding of gay dads and, as it turned out, fatherhood in general.[10]

As the father of three children and acquaintance of many other gay dads, Voeller was especially qualified to shed light on what Walters called "this little understood phenomenon." Voeller insightfully and patiently answered Walters's twenty-two questions, the first relating to the sheer possibility or existence of gay fathers. Voeller, a strong believer in pan-sexuality, explained that he, like most of his fellow gay dads, was "heterosexually competent" but leaned toward other males in terms of physical attraction. Some gay fathers like himself got divorced after having one or more children and became exclusively homosexual after their marriages ended. Most of the gay dads (and moms) Voeller knew were still married, however, with their spouses not aware of their mates' preferred sexuality. Married gays and lesbians felt a responsibility to their spouses and children, he explained, and stayed in their marriages despite the obvious conflict they felt. [11]

Voeller offered a wealth of other information related to gay fatherhood, answering questions many readers no doubt had about the little known subject. Homosexual dads did not wish their kids to be gay but would accept them if they were, he explained, and men who were attracted to those of their own gender were not necessarily more sensitive or feminine fathers than heterosexuals. The most important insights Voeller provided, however, had more to do with what could be considered universalities of parenthood, that is, the principles to which any good father or mother, regardless of sexual orientation or any other lifestyle choice, would subscribe. "I believe that the most fundamental thing a child can witness and learn is to be a loving and caring person," he told Walters, this being much more relevant than whether the father was homosexual or heterosexual. A good dad was a good dad, Voeller emphasized, his commitment to and relationship with his child the only thing that truly mattered. [12]

Voeller's observations were helpful, but some kind of qualitative or quantitative research was needed to gain a deeper understanding of gay fatherhood. The following year, the same journal published an article that broke additional new ground in the area of parenting by homosexual men. With his "Gay Fathers and Their Children," Brian Miller reported the results of a qualitative study he conducted among forty such men. This was the first empirical study to document the fathering abilities of gay men, laying a foundation for much more research to come in the 1980s. (The AIDS crisis stirred up significantly more interest in the lives of gay men in general.) In his article, Miller dispelled the myth that gay men had children to hide their homosexuality, and argued that fears of child sexual abuse by gay fathers or their gay friends was not warranted. Another key finding was that there was not a disproportionate amount of homosexuality among the children of gay fathers, an important point given the pronounced discrimination faced by such men in custody cases. Finally, contrary to popular belief, fathers do not expose their children to homophobic harassment, Miller learned. In sum, none of the widely held views about the alleged drawbacks to gay fatherhood were true, he reported. "People's sexual orientation says nothing about their desire or ability to care for children," Miller concluded, echoing Voeller's anecdotal information.[13]

CONVICTION, COURAGE, AND CASH

If gay fathers represented the hinterlands of sociological research in the 1970s, "bachelor" fathers were on the outskirts of town. Even in the early part of that decade—a time when virtually anything could and often did happen without too much social disapproval—the idea and reality of single fathers threw some for a loop. (Some believed it was not even legal for a single person to adopt children.) Dads whose wives died found themselves in such a position, as did divorcees who, against the odds, gained child custody. Adoption was another path for men without spouses to become fathers. More so than in the past, young, single, and successful men were choosing to adopt a child or two, with the circumstances for doing so varying widely. Some were Vietnam veterans who established an attachment for a certain orphaned boy or girl while overseas and returned after the war to adopt the child. (Many of these children were the offspring of American servicemen and Vietnamese women.) Other adopted children on moral grounds, taking in a "foundling" (an infant who had been abandoned by the parents) so that he or she would not grow up in an institution or be placed with an unfit family. Friends, neighbors, and family members typically helped out, a good thing given the new fathers' lack of experience in childcare. Some men would simply buy new clothes for an adopted child when the existing ones got dirty, being entirely unfamiliar with or loathing the process of doing laundry.[14]

It was divorce, however, that was fast becoming the primary reason for "bachelor" fathers, even if it was only on a part-time basis. In most states in the 1970s, mothers were almost by default awarded custody of children in divorce cases, with fathers granted visitation rights (typically every other weekend). Most disputes—as many as 90 percent—were settled out of court in meetings between each parent and his or her respective attorney. Taking history into consideration, it was usually ill advised for fathers seeking sole or joint custody to go to court.[15] Dads would often plead with judges to no avail, and walk out of courtrooms crushed by their demotion from parent to visitor. Other fathers made no attempt to gain primary or joint custody, knowing that the deck was strongly stacked against them. Most judges were especially leery of awarding custody of a daughter to a father, thinking dads knew little about raising a girl and that the living arrangement would be somehow unnatural.[16] Some women were known to diminish the childcare abilities of their husbands in order to increase the odds they would get custody, playing into judges' predispositions.[17]

For Daniel D. Molinoff, divorcing fathers needed three things—"conviction, courage, and cash"—if they intended to be awarded joint or sole custody of their children. Molinoff was an attorney who had gained joint custody of his two kids by proving his case in court and became somewhat of a spokesman for the cause. Over the course of America's first century, men were considered to "own" their children, legally speaking, but this began to change in the latter nineteenth century as women gained greater rights. By the turn of the twentieth century, mothers were routinely deemed the better caretaker and were more likely to gain custody of children in divorce cases. By the mid-1970s, years of litigation, weeks of trial, and ten to twenty thousand dollars in costs were likely required for men determined to challenge the prevailing system. As many contemporary fathers in troubled marriages know, moving out of the house or apartment was usually a bad idea if one wanted to retain custody of children, as judges tended to view that as a form of abandonment. Fathers who did move out usually rented a place as close as possible to where their kids still lived to make it easier to see them. Some women moved hundreds of miles away from where the family had lived, making that impossible.[18]

In addition to not leaving home, it was important for fathers to sue for divorce first as a preemptive strike in the war over the kids, Molinoff advised. Such a move ensured that the father would be designated as plaintiff (versus defendant) in the case, a key advantage if only for the tone it set. Getting a lawyer with matrimonial law expertise was also critical; too many men hired a friend whose specialty was in a different legal area, and later regretted the decision. Some of those who followed Molinoff's aggressive recommendations succeeded in their quest to win exclusive custody, with more on the way. "In a society that has long insisted that women are biologically better suited to raise children, these men—taking a cue from the feminist revolution of the 60's—have made 'fatherhood' a rallying cry of the 70's," he proudly declared in 1977. Almost nine hundred thousand American children under the age of eighteen lived with their male parent in 1974, a figure that was increasing as the number of divorces continued to grow.[19]

Divorce rates were skyrocketing despite the fact that only being married ensured fathers that they would be able to live with their children. One in three marriages was ending in divorce in the mid-1970s, as unhappy couples who might have stayed together in the past for "the sake of the children" no longer did so. Now children effectively "belonged" to the mother, according to the current judicial system, a by-product of two powerful forces: one, the traditional belief that women made better, more natural mothers; and two, the push by courts to affirm the rights of women and other historically marginalized groups. Interestingly, in many states the law itself made no distinction between parents in custody cases, but in courtrooms it was an entirely different matter. Fathers were simply less fit to be the custodial parent, most judges ruled, their principal role being to provide money to support the family. This was true even if the mother held a full-time job, an increasing likelihood at the time. The heavy bias toward women was all the more striking given that the vast majority of judges in the 1970s were men and, likely, fathers, and were thus aware of most dads' emotional attachment to children and their resolve to do whatever it took to raise them in the best way possible.[20]

THE MOTHERHOOD MYSTIQUE

Because they were so rare at the time, cases in which fathers pursued custody of their child caught the public's attention. In Boston in 1973, for example, an unwed father petitioned a court to gain custody of his son after the mother had given up the boy for adoption, shocking some for its unorthodoxy. With his act, the man became a local hero as he waged a vigorous, two-year legal battle to get the boy back. There was no precedent for what the father was attempting to do, however, and the court ruled that the boy should remain with his adoptive parents. It was impossible for an unwed father to provide "what's best for the child," the Supreme Judicial Court of Massachusetts ruled, keeping with tradition. Happily, some good did come out of the unusual case. The kerfuffle stirred Massachusetts lawmakers to consider giving unmarried fathers some rights in claiming their "illegitimate" children, an idea that would accelerate nationwide in the decades ahead.[21]

As more men raised kids without a mother, however, the idea of bachelor fatherhood gained greater acceptance. There was even a book on the subject: Michael McFadden's *Bachelor Fatherhood: How to Raise and Enjoy Your Children as a Single Father*. In his 1974 book, McFadden told men that fatherhood and fulfillment outside the home were not mutually exclusive concepts, something many single dads were no doubt happy to hear.[22] Despite the hard work, single fathers were finding parenting to be rewarding, a much different and more positive experience than the one they had had within their troubled marriage. Leisure time had become "kid time," and solo dads' cooking skills had made remarkable improvement with lots of practice. If a friend, neighbor, or family member was not available, a nanny, usually a local high school girl, could be found for some much-needed assistance. Children in single-parent households typically adjusted to the circumstances and became more self-sufficient, independent, and responsible people by being on their own more. Although a household in which both a mother and father was present was generally considered the ideal, research showed that children could indeed thrive with divorced but low-conflict parents who were each involved in their kids' lives. Given that good news, many psychologists were thus not overly concerned about men going it alone. "There is no scientific basis whatever to indicate that the female is superior to the male in doing this," said Dr. Lee Salk, director of pediatric psychology at the New York Hospital–Cornell Medical Center, the only exception being breastfeeding.[23]

The rise in single fatherhood in the 1970s had much to do with the growing number of social and economic options for women. The women's movement of the late sixties and early seventies helped make it significantly more permissible for mothers to opt out of being the primary caregiver to a child in divorce cases. As late as the mid-twentieth century, mothers who did not want to raise their children were considered heartless or perhaps insane, their feelings seen as going against Nature itself. (There must have been many divorce cases in which mothers reluctantly took their children against the wishes of fathers only because that was what society expected.) Although it may now seem obvious, it was not the gender of the parent but what a parent could bring to the child-raising experience that was important. It took until the mid-1970s for there to be a general understanding that love (versus gender) was the driving force of parenting, and that fathers were just as good at providing it as mothers. Even single fathers were capable of being excellent parents if, for whatever reason, they were in the position of being able to offer greater love to a child. More of them were getting that opportunity as stereotypical gender roles eroded. With 60 percent of women employed in some way in 1975, it was getting more difficult to justify mothers getting custody of a child in divorce cases simply on the basis of being the only full-time parent.[24]

Having gained some momentum and with gender roles increasingly amorphous, more determined fathers (some of them lawyers) losing custody battles in court decided to fight back. "If enough fathers are willing to do that, more and more fathers will win," reasserted Molinoff, urging that more men involved in custody disputes not just roll over.[25] In state after state, angry dads convinced that women were receiving favorable treatment in custody cases filed suits against the courts. In New Jersey in 1977, for example, a group of fathers presented evidence that women won custody 98 percent of the time in that state and were awarded far more hours of time with children than dads. Children of divorced couples spent an average of 158 hours a week with their mothers and just ten with their fathers, the group claimed, an amazing disparity that was likely representative of the nation as a whole. Parents had become playmates, the coalition of fathers told the State Superior Court of New Jersey, severely weakening the possibility of any kind of meaningful relationship with their respective children. One man in that state had made no less than seventy-nine court appearances over the course of just a few months to try to win back more time with his three kids, an indication of how resolute some were to change the unfair system.[26]

Interestingly, most of the men pursuing this path were going it alone. Hiring a lawyer was expensive (especially if dozens of court appearances were necessary), and many attorneys were reluctant to sue the very court system in which they regularly operated. Fathers were having a tough time at it in this early stage of what could be justifiably considered a men's movement to gain equal rights for custody of their children. Average dads knew little about court procedure and judicial matters, reason enough for many cases to be thrown out on technical grounds. In New Jersey, however, different groups of fathers were starting to band together, recognizing they would have more clout as an alliance than as lawyer-less individuals. The argument the men made was a powerful one: the ways courts were applying custody laws were discriminatory and unconstitutional, depriving divorced fathers equal rights protected by the Fourteenth Amendment.[27]

More precisely, judges were not interpreting or following the law as written, subscribing to what one of the New Jersey litigants called "the motherhood mystique." Custody rulings were based on assumptions that were antiquated if they were ever true at all, the father asserted, rightfully bitter that he hardly ever saw his children. After he and his wife divorced, the man was awarded the standard every-other-weekend visitation rights. Soon, however, his son lost interest in spending even this little amount of time with his dad—a prime example of fathers' inability to establish a healthy relationship with a child based on current custody practices. Alternate custody on a weekly, monthly, semiannual, or annual basis would be a much better policy for both fathers and children, men in this position contended, conveying to all involved parties that the family may have been separated but it had not been destroyed.[28]

FATHERS FOR EQUAL JUSTICE

Admittedly, there were cases in the mid-1970s where a father was awarded permanent custody of a divorcing couple's children. In 1975, Dr. Lee Salk (younger brother of Jonas) won his custody court battle, at least in part because he was perhaps the most professionally qualified father in the country. With his prominent position in the field and as author of the bestseller *What Every Child Wants His Parents to Know*, Salk had as good a case as could be made for being what the law termed a "fit" parent. In the vast majority of cases, it was only if the mother was considered "unfit" that the father was granted custody. In fact, a mother was often still awarded custody even if there was clear evidence that the she was somehow "unfit" due to misconduct, emotional instability, alcoholism, or neglect. The view that mothers who voluntarily gave up custody were abandoning their children had not completely disappeared, a sign of how entrenched standard parental roles were at the time. If men were considered to "own" their children in antebellum times, women were believed to possess them in the latter part of the twentieth century, almost as if they were a form of property.[29]

With his resume, however, Salk had a virtually unbeatable position over his ex-wife before the State Supreme Court of New York acting judge. Salk's ex-wife was not at all unfit, but it was the father who better served the emotional needs of their children, the judge declared, not too surprising given the man was an expert in all parental matters. While certainly unusual, this line of thought was the basis for most cases in which the father was awarded custody rights, giving less-than-famous men hope that they too would prove victorious in the courtroom or at least be given joint or equal time with their kids. Also helping men win custody fights was when they told judges they would be full-time fathers. Some men with an infant or toddler made it clear they would put their careers on hold for a couple of years in an attempt to convince a judge predisposed to awarding custodial rights to a stay-at-home mother to reconsider his decision. (Having considerable money in the bank to be able to do just that was also helpful.) More open-minded judges were also paying attention to the wishes of the involved child or children themselves, asking them (privately) whom they would prefer as a primary parent. (Such was the case in the celebrated Salk situation.) Court-appointed psychologists or psychiatrists were sometimes brought in by judges to help them make their decision, with shrinks often interviewing each member of the family to form their opinion.[30]

The traction men were making in custody fights extended to other negotiable parts of divorce settlements. More dads across the country were demanding they have a say in which educational, religious, and career paths their children took, if only in exchange for the alimony and child support they were required to pay. Fathers also wanted access to their children's medical and educational records, sensibly arguing that having them was important should a worrisome health- or school-related issue arise. (Some private schools were consenting to divorced dads' requests to receive a copy of their kid's report card.) It only made sense that fathers who loved their children wanted to spend a fair amount of time with them, but there was often more behind custody battles. Men intuitively knew that their children needed them as much as they needed their mothers, and this instinctive belief was backed up by a growing amount of research indicating the same. Children without fathers did not do as well in school as those who did have a dad around, according to early studies in the field, yet more reason for judges to take men's pleas seriously.[31]

Men's efforts to be good fathers despite the failure of their marriages were paying off in the late seventies. More than eighty groups of divorced fathers across thirty states had been formed by 1977, each one striving for equal rights for men in custody situations. Women were not always the victims of divorce and men always the instigators, members of groups such as Fathers for Equal Justice wanted the courts (and public) to know, meaning the latter should not automatically lose their parental rights when the couple decided to split up. Men had to demonstrate a kind of burden of proof that they were the better parent in court cases, something women did not have to do because of the prevailing "maternal mystique." As well, mothers sometimes did not allow their exes to see their children as visitation agreements stipulated, another beef among men in the ever-growing movement.[32]

With 1.7 million official divorces in the United States and many thousands of separations, it was not surprising to find significant variance in the terms of child custody. Some dads had the kids every other weekend, others every weekend, and still others no weekends at all. By 1977, women were getting custody 90 percent of the time on a nationwide basis, according to the *Journal of Divorce*, a sign of some progress but hardly the equal playing field men deserved. (That there even was such a journal was perhaps a commentary on the times.) Bickering couples typically created considerable tension in a household, leading to a stressful climate for all. Therapy and "divorce counseling" were routine for family members going through the painful process, especially among men who, after the breakup, felt alienated from their children.[33]

Divorce also had serious health consequences for men, new research showed, with those going through it twice as likely to die from heart disease, strokes, and cancer. Divorced men also had high rates of hypertension and cirrhosis, and were five times as likely to commit suicide. Even driving a car was more dangerous for men who had split from their wives, having three times the fatality rate of married men.[34]

Divorce carried a high physical price for fathers, but there were major financial and social consequences as well. A big chunk of men's income went to alimony and child support (sometimes more than 50 percent), requiring a significant downgrade in lifestyle for all but the rich. Most divorce settlements stipulated that alimony payments would stop should the woman remarry, making many men dream that happy day would come and come soon. It was a cliché, but a good number of divorced fathers really did live in small, cheap apartments chosen for both price and location. Staying in the neighborhood was important given how much else had changed in the men's lives, and being near the ex again made it easy for the kids to visit.[35]

The adverse effects of divorce upon men could be seen as compounding the palpable sense that fathers, even in the best of circumstances, remained peripheral parents throughout the 1970s. It was common for divorced men to see themselves as not just on the margins of parenthood but superfluous, a "guest" in the eyes of their children. Men were faced with the very difficult decision to try to maintain their existing, separated family, even with all its challenges, or seek to start a new one and leave the past behind.[36] The kind of relationship a father had with his ex had a lot to do with this decision, a 1978 research study on divorced parenthood showed; an amicable split was likely to lead to the former, an antagonistic one the latter.[37] Some men who had every intent of continuing their relationships with their children after a divorce soon gave up because of strong resistance from their ex-spouse and the court system. A portion of this group was willing to take on any obstacle to visitation rights but felt it would be better for the children if they gracefully bowed out because of the conflict involved. This was all the more sad when fathers had no doubt they were the more caring and nurturing parent.[38]

There were a myriad of other problems associated with divorce when children were involved. Picking up the kids from an ex- or soon-to-be-ex-wife's home was often an ugly, emotional affair, typically involving money, visitation schedules, or the issues that drove the couple apart. Things were even more likely to get dicey around holidays, children's birthdays, or when either parent was trying to schedule a vacation.[39] Living alone also was not easy for men used to being in a house or apartment filled with people, even if things were not going well. Fathers in such a position found themselves working very late, going to movies, drinking in bars, hanging out with friends, or doing anything else to avoid being by oneself in a depressingly quiet, often shoddy rental. While men longed for their exes to remarry for financial reasons, the thought of one's children having new fathers who supplanted them was truly devastating. Letters and phone calls were helpful to stay in touch, but another man's ability to tuck his children in bed every night was tough competition indeed.[40]

PARENTS WITHOUT PARTNERS

The thorny issue of custody cases was just one dimension of a rising interest in fatherhood, especially when divorce was involved. With separation and divorce reaching what were considered epidemic proportions in a historical sense, more sociologists were beginning to take a hard look at fathers when their marriages broke up. One 1978 study conducted by two Brandeis University sociologists and funded by the Rockefeller Foundation revealed key findings in what was a nascent area of study. (The researchers claimed that their study was the first to interview fathers, divorced or otherwise, in more than twenty years.) Kristine M. Rosenthal and Harry F. Keshet spoke with 127 Boston-area dads (most of them white, middle-class, and college-educated professionals in their thirties), with one key question in mind. "Who is happiest?" the researchers asked, dividing up the divorced fathers into three subgroups: full-time, half-time, and weekend parents. The answer to that question would shed considerable light on the impact of divorce upon men, the team believed, and lead to a greater understanding of the dynamics of family life in general.[41]

As perhaps might be expected, it was half-time divorced fathers who proved to be happiest in their lives, Rosenthal and Keshet found. Weekend fathers reported the time with their children was too limited and predetermined, while full-timers said their parental duties had severely cramped their social life. Half-timers also told the researchers they rarely experienced conflict with their exes and were inclined to become parents again should the opportunity present itself. There was, however, an interesting common denominator among all three subgroups of divorced fathers. Being a single parent encouraged if not forced men to become good nurturers, according to Rosenthal and Keshet, significantly more so in fact than while they were married. The absence of a mother appeared to bring out in single men a more sensitive side, in other words, an adaptive trait perhaps rooted in biology.[42]

The rise in single fatherhood prompted the publishing of a handful of useful books on the subject, such as Richard H. Gatley and David Koulack's *Single Fathers' Handbook: A Guide for Separated and Divorced Fathers*. While hardly an optimal state of affairs, a marital split offered kids the chance to live in two homes rather than just one, the authors pointed out, an interesting take on the difficult situation.[43] Edith Atkin and Estelle Rubin's *Part-Time Father* was also in the right place at the right time. The book helped show divorced dads without custody how they could maintain a relationship with kids they saw once a week at most, not an easy thing to do (especially when teenagers were involved). If there was any consolation, the authors told readers, most dads in perfectly stable marriages were "part-time fathers," meaning they did not spend much time with their kids. In fact, it was not unusual for the relationship between a father and child to improve after a marriage broke up, good news for dads thinking there was little or no hope of still being involved in their children's lives.[44] Recognizing divorce was a hot topic, publishers offered books about some aspect of it not just for adults but for children as well. For fifth to eighth graders, for example, there was *My Mother Is Not Married to My Father* (where mom got custody of the eleven-year-old protagonist, not surprisingly), while younger children could read *My Other-Mother, My Other-Father* (in which a child's parents remarry, making family life quite complicated for a girl).[45]

A subsegment of divorced dads—"weekend fathers"—were a conspicuous lot in these days when it was not common for married men to do activities with their kids without moms in tow. On any Saturday or Sunday in a large urban area, packs of such divorced men could be seen in parks, playgrounds, museums, and zoos, carrying on happily with their little ones. Squeezing in as much fun as possible into two days every two weeks was typically a frenetic affair for dad and tot alike, with any hint of boredom to be quashed as quickly as possible. Although most weekend fathers had become "weakened fathers" by Sunday night, most of them loved every minute of the limited visitation time they were granted in their divorce settlement. "You give your kids 100 per cent of your attention when you see them now," remarked Dan Isaacson, president of the Manhattan chapter of Parents Without Partners, "whereas before you probably took them for granted." Saying goodbyes on Sunday was often a difficult, tearful experience for all, especially for dads used to seeing their child or children day in, day out.[46] Dads might have been strict disciplinarians while they were married, but this typically changed after a divorce; the men were simply too grateful for the precious time spent together with their kids to admonish them for bad behavior.[47]

Divorce was rarely easy for a man or woman, even years after the split up, but it was typically the first few weeks or months that were the most difficult. With their relationship over, parenthood became increasingly important after divorce as it was the remaining connection to the family and loved ones.[48] Fathers experienced a range of emotions, with guilt perhaps the most disturbing. Dads felt they had failed not so much their partner but their children, regardless of who was actually more at fault. Growing up in a "broken home," as the saying went, could inflict all kinds of psychological damage upon children, and fathers felt and assumed much of the responsibility for putting them at such risk.[49]

Given the complications involved, it could be understood how post-divorce romance for both men and women was typically a challenge. "Starting over" or seeking love "the second time around," as the expressions went, were usually difficult pursuits for men more used to reading bedtime stories to children or helping them with homework at night than going on a date. Needless to say, the social scene in America was quite a different thing in the late 1960s and 1970s than it had been in the 1950s and early 1960s, when these men met the women they would ultimately marry and have children with. Some divorced fathers were intimidated by the kind of bolder woman now frequenting bars and clubs, while others were delighted about the sexual revolution that had taken place during their marital tenure. Some women avoided divorced fathers like the plague, not because they might be bad eggs but because they had little spending money after all they had to shell out to the ex.

Divorced fathers tended to go out with divorced mothers, a good arrangement both for financial reasons and the fact that there was usually no lull in conversations given they likely had some shared experiences.[50] Many men were in no hurry to remarry after their divorce, finding "dating around" to be perfectly sufficient given the less-than-sanguine results of their most recent serious relationship.[51]

THE VITAL COUNTERPART OF MOTHERING

Not surprisingly, the more conflicted domestic climate of the late sixties and seventies became a common theme in American popular culture. Producers of television shows, seeing an interesting twist on the traditional situation comedy, eagerly seized on the new image of fatherhood and, more generally, alternative expressions of family life. Divorce was still a touchy topic for network TV, justification to present single fathers as widowers (and earning the lead character empathy rather than scorn among female viewers). Such was the case in *My Three Sons*, *The Courtship of Eddie's Father*, and *Eight Is Enough* (with the lead character of the latter getting remarried). *The Brady Bunch* blazed new televisual territory with its portrayal of a blended family in which the father raised children originally not his own, while *Family Affair* was about a father raising his brother's orphaned kids. And if dads acted the fool in the fifties as comic relief, some fathers in 1970s sitcoms plainly did not always "know best." Cracks in the paternal foundation of the American family can clearly be seen in *Bewitched*, *All in the Family*, *Good Times*, *The Jeffersons*, *Soap*, and *Mary Hartman, Mary Hartman*, with the father in all these shows not just feckless but somehow flawed.

The foibles of Archie Bunker or George Jefferson were certainly humorous, but fatherhood was intersecting with a number of serious social issues in the 1970s. A notable one was abortion, which remained a contentious site even as laws regulating the procedure were passed. Neither *Roe v. Wade* or *Doe v. Bolton*, each a landmark abortion case from 1973, had anything of substance to say about the rights of biological fathers, leaving the matter unclear. Did fathers' rights extend to unborn children? If so, how would those rights relate to a woman's now legal right to terminate her pregnancy? Legal scholars asked such questions, with a growing number of abortion cases forcing judges at all levels to reach some sort of an opinion. Potential fathers were contesting abortions, claiming that they would be denied the benefits of parenthood should the mother's decision be honored. Such a case was filed in New Jersey in 1977, for example, with that state's Supreme Court blocking an abortion planned by a woman after her "male friend" argued it would violate his right to future fatherhood. A Superior Court judge and a state appeals court had previously rejected the man's plea, but the New Jersey Supreme Court believed the matter deserved full consideration.[52] Other men who did not want to be fathers because of the legal and financial obligations claimed they had an equal say in whether the mother should have an abortion. Such claims challenged women's control over their own bodies, however, which had been the fundamental basis for the decision in *Roe v. Wade*. Until there was more legal precedent, judges were treating the issue much like conflicts relating to adoption, that is, on a case-by-case basis.[53]

Another important issue relating to the rights of fathers revolved around the birth of their children. In the early 1970s, a good number of hospitals across the country began offering "father's hour" to men who had just become dads (like natural childbirth, an early attempt to bring men into the pregnancy process). Most new fathers were afraid to even touch their newborns, not surprisingly given the literally hands-off role men were expected to play with infants. But that was beginning to change as more innovative healthcare professionals understood the contribution fathers could make to the development of their children. More fathers were being encouraged to join mothers at their baby's feeding time and actually join in if a bottle was needed. Dads were also urged to change their baby's diapers, another relatively new thing at the time. Men had long attended child-rearing classes, but taking part in the real thing represented a big shift in the care of newborns. Long left to view their babies through glass windows, proud papas were now (nervously) holding them soon after birth in order to immediately establish a close familial bond. Most men quickly learned to recognize distress signals sent by their infants, as fast in fact as mothers, for whom it was assumed to be natural. Fathers may not have been able to breastfeed, but it was becoming increasingly clear that hospital "maternity wards" might have to change their names as dads became part of the childbirth process.[54]

The breakthrough realization that new dads could hold and care for their newborns without disastrous results made researchers want to know more about the possibilities of fatherhood. Fathers played with infants more and differently than mothers, they noted, an observation that would become a common theme in parenthood literature for decades to come. Moms were happy to play peek-a-boo and pat-a-cake with babies, but that was simply not enough for men wanting more physical interaction. Researchers were also establishing a link between the relative involvement of a father and a child's social responsiveness. Infants who had considerable interaction with their dads were not especially upset when left in a room with a stranger, for example, while those who had not exhibited great distress. Fathers also helped little ones develop cognitively, studies were beginning to show, with more contact the better. "Fathers play a unique and important role in infancy," wrote Ross D. Parke in *Sciences* in 1979, correctly predicting that men would take on a significantly larger role in their children's lives in the years ahead.[55]

The changes taking place in more progressive hospitals would soon be reflected in scholarly literature dedicated to fatherhood. Books such as editor Michael E. Lamb's *The Role of the Father in Child Development* (1976) and Marshall L. Hamilton's *Father's Influence on Children* (1977) took an interdisciplinary approach in documenting dads' significant impact upon the identity, morality, and sociability of their kids. As well, more attention was being paid to the detrimental effects of non-fatherhood, that is, how children suffered when their dads were not around.[56] A backlash against the liberalities of the counterculture was clearly in the works around the time of the nation's bicentennial, ushering in a more conservative expression of fatherhood. "Modern man does not seem to have deviated far from the centuries-old conception of what he is supposed to do as father," wrote Joseph W. Maxwell in *Family Coordinator* in 1976, believing that we should reacknowledge dads' time-honored role as family provider. News of the death of the American nuclear family was premature, he proclaimed, happy to report that there were still men who subscribed to a traditional interpretation of paternity.[57]

The expansion of fatherhood in the latter 1970s could thus be seen as one dimension of a larger cultural shift taking place in the country. An explosion of popular books and articles on the subject were now being published, making it quite apparent that some kind of corner in parenting and the country itself was being turned. America was clearly coming out of its early seventies funk, with everyone happy to see the end of the traumatic events of the last few years—"stagflation," the energy crisis, the Watergate debacle, and the Vietnam War. As well, the "anything goes" attitude of the last decade was in fast decline, eclipsed by a more traditional social and cultural climate despite the meteoric rise of Democratic presidential candidate Jimmy Carter. (Carter's appeal was more populist than liberal, buttressed by his background as a peanut farmer and Navy man.) The idea of "family values" was in ascent, an ideology that would take serious hold in a few years with the equally spectacular climb of neoconservative Ronald Reagan.

Buoyed by this new kind of commitment to family life, the gender blurring associated with the counterculture naturally seeped into the concept and practices of fatherhood. Fathers were taking on more responsibilities for childcare precisely when great numbers of women embarked on careers, a historic shifting of gender roles. Fathers were essentially adopting the model of parenting established by mothers, that is, a feminine approach that left little room for any kind of expression of masculinity. Dads of this period were raised by fathers of the postwar generation whose breadwinning and authoritative capabilities were generally far superior to their capacity for nurturance. With no other viable parental platform to go by, it made perfect sense for dads of the 1970s to look to moms for inspiration in all childcare matters. This style of parenting, which would soon become known as "the new fatherhood," was radical, perhaps revolutionary at the time for its embrace of maternal love and devotion to one's children. It would take another generation of fathers to exchange this model for one that not only accommodated but celebrated masculinity within the domain of parenting.

With little actual experience in such matters, many men relied on experts to guide them through the alien realm of parenting. Books such as Fitzhugh Dodson's *How to Father* (1974), Henry Biller and Dennis Meredith's *Father Power* (1975), and Sara D. Gilbert's *What's a Father For?* (1975) appeared on bookshelves, each offering men useful tips on the raising of children. These books were most notable for their feminine take on fatherhood, that is, that dads' best route to successful parenting would be to adopt their wives' techniques. *How to Father* made no distinction between fathering and mothering, its author arguing that the basic principles of good parenting had no real gender basis.[58] *Father Power* urged men to rid themselves of their patriarchal instincts and instead cultivate parenting techniques rooted in sensitivity and tenderness, while *What's a Father For?* endorsed the elimination of gender differences in childcare wherever possible.[59] Self-help and alternative psychological therapies were all the rage at the time, of course, each of these movements no doubt informing popular views on parenting.

A FATHERLESS SOCIETY

While a wonderful thing, the progress men were making in the mid-1970s as actively engaged fathers was more of a whisper than a bang. The seeds of the new fatherhood had been planted, but it would take time for them to blossom into a full-fledged movement. Fatherhood in America remained the target of considerable criticism, much of it deserved. Maureen Green's 1976 *Fathering* was a particularly vitriolic attack on uninvolved or missing dads. Green, an avowed feminist, raised a number of controversial issues related to fatherhood in her book, including the question of whether fathers were "America's newest endangered species." Green was happy to see that fathers had lost much of their patriarchal power, largely in part due to women's rising economic clout. Fathers' role in family life had become uncertain with their weaker social status, she argued, leading her to suggest that they may indeed become extinct or treated like "pets" by their wives and children. Given the strides American fathers had recently made, Green's thesis was debatable, or at least somewhat dated. The author had done her homework, however, studying the available academic literature in the subject to learn that fathers did indeed make a positive contribution in the raising of children when they had the opportunity to do so. Boys and girls were more likely to grow up to be emotionally stable, happy, and well-educated adults when a father was around, research showed, meaning they should not be completely given up on. Instead, Green advised men to assert their role within the family and take full advantage of their inherent capacity to improve the well-being of their kids.[60]

Other women urged men to take equal responsibility as parents, seeing the latter's ability to provide emotional support as just as important as providing financial assistance. Women were especially attuned to the contributions fathers made to the development of daughters and thus tended to be vigorous advocates for the new, more nurturing dad who was emerging in the late seventies. On Father's Day 1978, for example, Women's Way, an organization founded in Philadelphia in the mid-1970s to enhance the lives of women, petitioned men to be just as good parents to daughters as to sons. Many fathers simply did not have the emotional tools to do that, but they were receptive to acquiring them. In fact, open-minded men were joining "consciousness-raising" groups to become more familiar with the historical oppression of women, an area of study that would serve them well as fathers. Getting in touch with one's own feelings and learning how to share them with other men was another objective of these male get-togethers that were popular in the therapy-happy 1970s.[61]

Men too suggested that fatherhood still had a long way to go if they expected to be treated as equal partners in parenting. William Reynolds's *The American Father: A New Approach to Understanding Himself, His Woman, His Child* from 1978 was a downright depressing portrayal of fatherhood and family life in general. Reynolds, a psychologist, presented men and women as essentially incompatible within a domestic setting, with each party wanting different things in life. After keeping all the balls of the family juggling act in the air, moms had little time for anything else, including dads, he argued. (Reynolds was the father of seven children, which perhaps informed his dark point of view.) Fathers, meanwhile, often acted like the needy children they were supposed to be nurturing, not a pretty picture for anyone.[62] Based on this kind of analysis, it was surprising that all couples had not gone their separate ways.

All agreed that the worst kind of fathers were those who had abandoned their families. Some of these men were keeping the public assistance money intended for their families, making them not just irresponsible but villainous. Throughout the 1970s, a concerted effort was made by city, state, and federal elected officials to track down fathers who had left their families while still getting welfare checks. Early attempts to solve the problem failed because the programs were understaffed, underfunded, and poorly managed. (New York State went as far as to hire an FBI agent to try to catch the deserters.)[63] But with a new law enacted by Congress in 1976, welfare officials believed they now had the resources to literally get their man. The goal was to recover the money the ne'er-do-wells received from the government, which in aggregate was no small change. One billion dollars a year was paid out to married or unwed fathers who had abandoned their children, a figure that would make it well worth the extra manpower. Key to the new program was a Federal Parent Locator Service that provided access to all national and state records, including Social Security, IRS, and military service information. Federal employees were at particular risk of getting nabbed, with their wages to be garnished if caught.[64]

The accelerating rate of absenteeism became a metaphor for the generally sorry state of fatherhood in the 1970s. Some argued that the country had become "a fatherless society" or was rapidly headed that way, a byproduct of the deterioration of paternal authority (as well as religious morality) since the end of World War II. The result was an unhealthy attraction to mass culture among young people, expressed through the shallow pursuits of consumerism and conformity.[65] Conversations with men were indeed likely to reveal that the relationships with their own fathers had been weak while they were growing up. This generation of fathers had, after all, been raised in the 1950s by men who were not known for readily expressing love for their children. "Very few sons remember being fondled, held or kissed by fathers on a daily basis," wrote Phyllis Chesler in the *New York Times* in 1978, thinking that men recall "liking" their dads more than loving them. (The opposite was true of mothers.) Often not at home, prone to emotional aloofness, and inclined to physicality when discipline was required, the postwar generation of men were not good role models for fathers interested in establishing an especially close relationship with their children.[66]

Still, there was cause to be optimistic about the future of fatherhood as the chaotic 1970s drew to a close. Fatherhood in America was in major transition, after all, with a new importance and recognition attached to the role dads played in family life. These changes were not taking place in a vacuum, of course, reshaping the overall parenting process and, more generally, adults' relationships with children. "The shift seems part of a pervasive reordering of the family system with changes in social definitions of male and female roles," Bradley Soule, Kay Standley, and Stuart A. Copans observed in *Psychiatry* in 1979, understanding that nothing short of a kind of domestic revolution was at work. Much attention had been paid to the social and political upheaval associated with the counterculture over the past decade and a half, but relatively little to the degree to which parenting had been recreated. Over the past century in America, parenting had been almost synonymous with mothering, but this was quickly changing as fathers reinvented their place in family life. Just as the feminist movement was altering the marital equation between men and women, so was this new kind of fatherhood transforming spousal relationships. Men's identity too was evolving, representing a fundamental restructuring of the dynamics of gender.[67]

If there was any sign to be bullish on fatherhood, it took place on April 30, 1979. Father's Day had been around for decades, of course, but that year President Jimmy Carter felt the need to declare the day officially. Fathers were now expected to play a more significant role in raising children, he noted, calling upon dads to take on greater responsibilities in family life. Carter and his wife had four children, and the couple made concerted efforts to be actively involved parents despite their very busy schedules (something President Barack Obama and First Lady Michelle Obama would also do a few administrations later). With his speech, the president publicly acknowledged the importance and value of fatherhood in America, a sentiment that would only increase in the coming decade.[68] Fatherhood had had a rough time in recent years, but this was to change dramatically as the nation headed into the 1980s.

2

THE NEW FATHERHOOD

My brain is like oatmeal. I yelled at Kenny today for coloring outside the lines! Megan and I are starting to watch the same TV shows, and I'm liking them! I'm losing it.
—Jack Butler, played by Michael Keaton in the 1983 movie *Mr. Mom*

In 1981, Anatole Broyard observed what he considered to be the renaissance of fathers in the Great American Novel. Between the 1950s and early 1970s, fathers "shrank" in fiction, the writer and literary critic suggested, citing characters in Bruce Jay Friedman's *A Mother's Kisses*, Thomas McGuane's *Ninety-Two in the Shade*, and Philip Roth's *Portnoy's Complaint* as examples of this diminishing of fatherhood. Fathers in these novels were weak, foolish, and vain, their authors (all male) perhaps using what many agreed was the demasculinization of American society as inspiration. But recently published novels had reversed the trend, Broyard believed, thinking it was the mid-1970s when fathers "began to get color in their cheeks again." Characters in Donald Barthelme's *The Dead Father*, William Maxwell's *So Long, See You Tomorrow*, William Wiser's *Disappearances*, and Barry Targan's *Kingdoms* all reflected the emotional and psychological revival of fathers in contemporary fiction. "It is as if fathers are returning home again, being welcomed back from exile," Broyard concluded, with novelists using their characters "to explain themselves to themselves."[1]

Broyard's observations about a recent transformation in fatherhood went well beyond the literary world. As the first wave of baby boomers began to have children en masse in the mid-1970s, a noticeable change in how men acted as parents could be detected. Now backed by the more conservative, family-oriented cultural climate of what would come to be known as the Reagan Era, fatherhood in America was clearly on a new and different track than that of the counterculture years. Many dads were happily (or so it seemed) participating in the births of their children, changing diapers, and bathing babies, all things that men of previous eras were not known for. The image of the American dad as "remote breadwinner" was rapidly being replaced by a style of fatherhood grounded in affection and attachment as younger men embraced an alternative role in family life. Just as some women were being referred to as "supermoms" as they pursued both motherhood and full-time careers, some men were beginning to be labeled "superdads" for their active and, often, zealous participation in work and parenthood.[2] This model of male parenting would be summarily described as "the new fatherhood," a method or approach in which men looked to women for inspiration when it came to raising children. As "the new fatherhood" became entrenched in American society, it was apparent that male identity in general was experiencing a major transition. Both men and women were challenging traditional gender roles, in the process redefining everyday life in the United States.

A NEW DEAL

Soon after the Reagans moved into the White House, the idea of "a new fatherhood" gained considerable traction in popular discourse. Not surprisingly, *Parents* magazine, the leading voice of parenthood in the United States, consistently (and happily) reported stories about this historical shift in childcare and masculinity. Thirty-plus years later, it is difficult to fully appreciate the significance assigned to the new role of fathers in the early 1980s. Dads were routinely bathing, changing, and serving as principal playmate to their toddlers, a radical development that few could have predicted in the not-very-paternalistic 1970s. Men in suits at work could be found discussing which brands of diapers to use and avoid, a topic that likely would not have been brought up just a few years earlier. Baby carriers for men had become a ubiquitous sight in urban areas, with proud fathers' bulging bellies looking not unlike those of pregnant mothers. The image served as an apt metaphor for the new responsibilities fathers had taken on, tasks that ideally matched those of mothers as closely as possible. That the change was not merely stylistic but substantive was perhaps the most remarkable thing about "the new fatherhood"; the attitudinal and behavioral transformation of men challenged many of the suppositions about the dynamics of both family and gender.[3]

The mainstream media eagerly reported the big news that fatherhood in America had been transformed into something new and different. The dual raising of children was, according to *Newsweek* in 1981, "a new deal," something "being struck in an increasing number of American households." Social and economic forces were converging to elevate the responsibilities of and opportunities for fathers, the magazine told readers, and the rules of parenting were being rewritten in the process. Fathers were a lot more like mothers than previously believed, experts now agreed, the concept of masculinity increasingly infused with traits like sensitivity and tenderness. As a result, the nation was experiencing something of a "father fixation," *Newsweek* noted, with a growing number of how-to books, classes, and workshops dedicated to improving the fatherhood experience. Mostly dormant over the past generation, fathers had rather suddenly reawakened, charged now with being every bit as much an involved parent as mothers. While more traditional (usually less affluent) men were less likely to embrace what they saw as "women's work," and some mothers were resistant to giving up their role as primary caregiver in the family, "the trend is clear," the magazine observed. The "50-50 family" was on the rise, something few could have ever predicted given the history of gender not just in this country but in virtually all others.[4]

Fittingly, then, the notion of "the expectant father" became part of the trope of "the new fatherhood." Stories of men going to their doctors complaining of abdominal pain, weight gain, fatigue, and anxiety were frequently heard, the common denominator being that the patients were all soon going to be fathers. Almost 25 percent of "expectant fathers" reported such symptoms, a recent study by the University of Rochester found, with doctors typically failing to connect the complaints to their partners' pregnancy. The condition even had a real, medical name—couvade syndrome—with nausea, vomiting, cramps, and bloatedness, among other symptoms. In French, *couvade* means to cover, or sit on, eggs, with the syndrome prevalent across cultures. Psychiatrists had no problem coming up with potential psychological causes for men sharing the common physical discomforts of pregnant women, including sympathy, identification, and stress, but there were few useful treatments for the odd condition. "An expectant father should consider the possibility that his body is trying to tell him something, and he should try to figure out what the pregnancy means to him and to his relationship with his wife," advised physicians Paula Adams Hillard and J. Randolph Hillard, words of little comfort for men wondering why they had suddenly become rather pudgy and were tired all the time.[5]

One did not have to be a psychiatrist or physician to know that, just like moms, dads typically experienced mixed feelings or ambivalence about parenthood in the months after having a child. Emotions swing wildly with a newborn, ranging from exhilaration to the "baby blues," or postpartum depression. If there was any single emotion outside of joy that came with being a new father, however, it very well may have been fear. Seeing firsthand the level of care that a baby needed, as well as the amount of money that would be required in the years ahead, often brought on a state of pure terror among first-time dads. Fathers also felt conflicted about their new dual role, that of provider and caregiver. Spending time with a newborn was both enjoyable and trying, interesting and boring, and satisfying and frustrating. When at home, especially after a tough session with baby, some fathers wished they were in the more predictable and orderly universe of work; while at work, they longed to see their child's smile. This sense of being caught between two worlds would recede after some time but never completely go away, just one way things would, as many veteran fathers had warned, never be quite the same after becoming a dad.[6]

Because of their ever-growing involvement as parents, fathers of the early 1980s were likely more prone to experience this kind of ambivalence than those of past generations, or at least admit to such. "I love my little girl an extraordinary amount," proclaimed Harry Stein in *Esquire* in 1981, while also confessing, "there have been moments when I've wanted nothing more than to flee the house and hop the first plane headed anywhere." Stein was bothered by the rather new expectation for fathers to feel "tingly and warm and perpetually giddy," with any deviation from such judged as not just sad but abnormal. Worse, Stein was finding himself adopting the same kind of expectations, feeling guilty when he realized he was not being a perfect dad in some way. Other fathers (and mothers) were in a similar place, he learned after asking around, thinking that the social pressure to be an ideal parent was unreasonable and unhealthy. After having a first child, many dads and moms were reconsidering their plan to have another, finding that one was more than enough given the absurdly high bar that was set by both themselves and others. New fathers were reluctant to admit any of this to others, with anything less than 100 percent commitment to parenthood treated as a kind of social taboo.[7]

Given Stein's refreshingly candid sentiment about parenthood, it was not surprising that a few years later he revealed his thoughts about what he called "second-child syndrome." Writing in the same publication, Stein shared his thoughts on his so-far-brief tenure with his newborn son, an experience he described as at least as ambivalent as that with his first child. After becoming a father again, Stein felt the need to reprise his controversial view that parenthood was a decidedly mixed bag. While the time he had spent with his daughter over the past three and a half years was "the most gratifying, the most emotionally stimulating, of my life," he explained, the price paid in terms of his career was extremely high. Now having the flu that his daughter had brought home from school and getting just a few hours of his sleep because of the baby, Stein was more convinced than ever that being a good father inherently carried a heavy cost. There was a fundamental conflict between parenthood—an enterprise offering great joy but predicated on sacrifice—and work—an endeavor that was at its essence an expression of selfhood. Stein had always defined himself first and foremost as a writer; hence his discontent in falling short in that regard because of his new responsibilities. Parenthood was immensely rewarding but required one to give up a piece of one's former self, Stein was saying, something that many fathers (and certainly a good number of mothers) felt but would never have the courage to mention.[8]

Another writer, David Osborne, also felt the need to push back against what he called "the cult of fatherhood." (Perhaps because their jobs did not have the boundaries of those who worked nine to five, writers in general seemed to have a tough time dealing with the social expectations of being a "superdad.") His wife a physician who worked a hundred hours a week, Osborne was assigned the primary duty of taking care of both their toddler and their house. Like many other full-time dads, Osborne could not relate at all to the kind of fatherhood experience recently described by Bob Greene in his bestseller *Good Morning, Merry Sunshine: A Father's Journal of His Child's First Year*. Osborne wondered how any parent of a young child had the time to write a book, thinking that Greene's journaling was at best conveniently incomplete or, worse, largely a fabrication designed to cash in on the current fascination with "the new fatherhood." Beyond being "hopelessly in love" with his little boy, Osborne had precious few profound thoughts to share regarding his fatherhood experience, simply because he had no time or energy to construct them. For he and many others, fatherhood had become, in essence, their new full-time job.[9]

NOT ALL HYPE

Although certainly buoyed by the media, the new fatherhood did indeed represent a major historical shift in masculine identity. "The new father is not all hype," psychologist Joseph Pleck told *Parents* magazine in 1987, thinking that the phenomenon was "ultimately rooted in structural forces and structural changes." In a trio of books published over a dozen years—*Men and Masculinity* (1974), *The American Man* (1980), and *The Myth of Masculinity* (1981)—Pleck traced the role of fatherhood in America during the previous three centuries, putting this latest phase in valuable historical context. From the seventeenth century through the mid-nineteenth century, Pleck showed, fathers assumed the weighty role of a godlike figure, responsible for the moral compass of a family. Fathers instilled values in their children mostly through religion, and educated them so that they too could understand and appreciate the Scriptures.[10] A "good father" was one who guided his family based on the principles of "Christian living" and, as this 1844 poem illustrated, held a great degree of paternal authority:

> The father gives his kind command.
> The mother joins, approves;
> The children will attentive stand.
> Then each obedient moves.[11]

The second phase of fatherhood in America began in the mid-nineteenth century when the Industrial Revolution altered the trajectory of masculine identity, Pleck continued. As men increasingly migrated to jobs outside the home, their role in family life became primarily defined as financial provider. Through the 1930s, fathers viewed themselves and were viewed by others principally as breadwinners, with their wives in charge of homemaking and the raising of children. While they still offered moral guidance and possessed considerable authority in family matters, fathers' first order of business now was to earn money to support the household.[12]

It was during World War II when American fathers again assumed a different predominant identity, Pleck argued. During the war and postwar years, men held onto their moral and financial responsibilities but took on the greater purpose of serving as models of masculinity. Strict gender roles encouraged by a more traditional and conservative cultural climate pushed fathers to embrace characteristics of "maleness" that, importantly, contrasted with those of "femaleness." American society was becoming increasingly feminized, many (male) experts in the 1950s feared, reason enough for men to impart a maximum amount of masculinity to family life. Sons were the main focus of such efforts, with all kinds of psychological harm believed to await those boys who looked to women for personality and lifestyle cues. Fathers were widely ridiculed in popular culture during these years, not surprisingly, their alleged weaknesses exposed in everything from television shows like *I Love Lucy* to movies such as *Rebel Without a Cause* to comic strips like *Blondie*.[13]

The fourth and final phase of the American father emerged in the mid-1970s, according to Pleck (supporting Broyard's observation of the renaissance of men in fiction since then). The women's movement and parallel development of greater equality in the workplace lifted the status of men in family life, perhaps ironically, giving rise to the more active, involved, and nurturing father. The "good father" was now one who contributed heavily to the raising of children and, often, homemaking chores, a virtually total reversal from the nearly supreme identity of the American dad a century earlier. The seeds of "the new fatherhood" had been planted, its full blossoming now taking place in the increasingly child-friendly 1980s.[14]

Assuming the responsibilities of the new fatherhood came early, usually even before the child was born. Childbirth classes became increasingly popular among post-counterculture fathers, primarily as a means for men to demonstrate their full commitment to parenthood. As well, roughly 80 percent of American hospitals now allowed (and often encouraged) fathers to be present in the delivery room when their partner gave birth. (About half of men took doctors up on this offer, with another third opting for the safe haven of the waiting room.) There was some research indicating that the presence of fathers in the delivery room eased mothers' pain during labor, one reason why they were urged to be there. (In the early part of the twentieth century, it was grandmothers rather than fathers who were sometimes invited to take part in the birthing process, then more likely to be held in bedrooms than hospitals. In midcentury, fathers were frequently told by obstetricians to "go home and get a good night's sleep," an order they happily obeyed.)[15] Another reason for fathers to be present in the delivery room was the growing belief that men were more inclined to embrace the responsibilities of fatherhood after seeing their baby born, an interesting idea based at the time more on anecdotal evidence than empirical study.[16] Whether or not that was true, the United States was finally catching up to many other societies where fathers or another close relative accompanied the mother during labor. American dads were in some respect playing the role of a doula, a supportive companion who assists in birth in some cultures.[17]

The most central part of life—childbirth—had thus become something quite different in the United States than it had been in the postwar years. Fathers then were not only not in the delivery room but sometimes a hundred miles away, ready to greet their child a day or two (or more) after he or she was born. Childbirth was moms' responsibility, with dads playing little or no role in it except waiting for it to happen and, as everyone knew, passing out cigars when it was all over. As well, mothers were often under anesthesia during childbirth; they and their doctors saw no reason why there should be any pain involved now that it could be avoided. But now "natural," drug-free childbirth was common, with fathers taking part in the process by helping their partners breathe and relax as pain-reducing techniques. For both mothers and fathers, childbirth had become something to experience, a major life event to embrace rather than miss out on.[18]

By the mid-1980s, however, some parents were beginning to rethink the alleged joys of natural childbirth, wondering if there was something to their own mothers' reliance on good old-fashioned painkillers. While happy they had the chance to be in the delivery room (and often cut the umbilical cord), a good many dads had no desire to experience the sights and sounds that typically go into a natural birth of a child. Emotions run high while the baby makes its way out of a woman's vagina, these wide-ranging, unpredictable feelings often complemented by the din of primal screams that one will not soon forget. Women were known to ask their doctors for a sedative when the contractions intensified, but physicians would frequently refuse to administer one, not wanting to "de-naturalize" the planned birth. Fathers hated to see their partners suffer so much and realized they had no real control over the situation that had been months in planning. The latest trend was for not just dads but siblings to be present in the delivery room (an experience more skeptical fathers believed would take the brother or sister years of therapy to get over).[19]

The push, so to speak, for fathers to play a part in the birthing experience of their children sometimes ran to extreme measures. In an attempt to take immediate paternal bonding to the ultimate degree, a group of doctors in New Jersey in the late 1970s and early 1980s were encouraging fathers to actually deliver their children. By 1981, six hundred fathers had done exactly that at Washington Memorial Hospital in Turnersville as part of an initiative to make childcare more "family-centered" versus "mother-centered." If fathers were likely to become emotionally attached to their babies by being present during birth, the obstetricians held, they would become even more so by bringing them into the world themselves. Such a thing would have long-term benefits, the theory went, the literal beginning of a loving relationship between father and child for years to come. Nurses at the hospital were supportive of the idea and assisted the "laboring couple" in any way they could, even sometimes taking photos of the event.[20]

How the program at Washington Memorial Hospital began was as kooky as the very notion of fathers acting as obstetricians. The idea took root in 1974 when one dad-to-be jokingly asked one of the doctors if he could deliver his baby. After checking to see if such a thing was legal and getting approval from the hospital's head staff, the man was soon pulling his child from his wife's womb with only his doctor's instructions to guide him. More dads wanting to share the experience were soon signing up, with only a complication or need for a cesarean disqualifying them from donning gown and gloves and grabbing the baby from the mom's belly. No training was provided beforehand, rather incredibly, the justification being that this literal "hands on" approach was the way medical students learned how to deliver a baby. Daddies delivering babies was a lot safer than home deliveries, the real obstetricians justified their decision, with doctors and medical equipment right in the room should a problem develop. "Feeling the life in her was the greatest thing," said one father after delivering his daughter, claiming he did indeed sense an immediate and powerful attachment to the girl. Seven years after the program began, the trio of obstetricians was trying to prove their theory by following up with the couples who had taken part in it. Preliminary findings indicated that the program did have a host of positive outcomes on family life, but other doctors across the country were in no hurry to pass off their jobs to amateurs.[21]

A POOL OF PATERNAL YEARNINGS

Although fathers delivering their babies is obviously an extreme example, it signals the general elevation of men in family life in the 1980s. Fathers' gradual ascent to the lofty rank of co-parent ran parallel with hard research showing that men were not parentally handicapped from a biological sense. "Social rather than biological factors account for the major differences between men and women in parenting behavior," noted Ronna Kabatznick, a social psychologist, in *Ms.* magazine in 1984.[22] For a variety of reasons, it was difficult for men to shake the perception that they were physically disadvantaged when it came to caring for children, especially babies. "Historically," wrote Robert B. McCall, author of *Infants*, "dads have been regarded as irrelevant or even incompetent to care for a new baby." Fearing the worst, hospital staffs were reluctant to leave fathers alone with their newborns.[23] Mothers were long believed to be better caregivers than fathers because they were supposedly "hardwired" to react to a baby's sounds and movements, particularly those of distress. The truth was that fathers too had this natural instinct, however, with research also showing that men were not all thumbs when it came to feeding a baby with a bottle. Dads could bill and coo just as well as moms, it was also shown, the art of baby talk not limited to females. In short, men and women were much more alike than different as new parents, according to the latest studies, breaking down the traditional view that families would be best served by dads leaving infant care to mom. Playing with older kids was another story, however, with study after study showing that fathers leaned heavily toward the physical and mothers the verbal.[24]

More research indicating clear distinctions between mothers and fathers emerged in the early 1980s. One study presented at the 1983 annual meeting of the American Psychological Association confirmed, should there have been any doubt, that fathers' forte was playtime while mothers assumed a much broader array of childcare activities. Interestingly, dads' emphasis on tactile and physical interaction and moms' attention to everything else made children quite aware that males and females were different, University of Vermont psychologist Phyllis Bronstein told her colleagues. At a very early age, she reported, kids learned that women were omnipresent, attentive, and calming creatures while men offered intermittent excitement, a conclusion that carried through life. As a book published a decade later would declare, men were from Mars while women were from Venus, with these gender differences playing out not just in romance but in parenting.[25]

Paradoxically, perhaps, while greater distinctions were being made between mothers and fathers as parents, gender roles in another sense were becoming more fluid. As more women embarked on full-time careers in the 1980s, more men found themselves being full-time parents, a historic reversal in gender identities. For new dads thrust into the position of being the primary caretaker of their child, it was often on-the-job training. Some fathers had never previously picked up a baby, making them hold the little thing with a viselike grip. Men were typically surprised by how difficult being a parent of a newborn was, making them change their views about women who chose to be full-time moms instead of pursuing a career. Full-time fathers assigned the additional job of taking care of the house while mothers worked found themselves playing the role of the harried housedad sometimes seen in movies or on television, but without any of the humor. There was little funny about trying to answer the phone or doorbell while feeding the baby, these men quickly learned, especially when the toilet was overflowing or a pot was boiling over. The reality of no lunch or coffee break was also a rude awakening, ex-career men found, and the possibility that one's wife would have to work late was the stuff of nightmares. "No one would take a regular job like this," said one such full-time dad, considering his new position "inhumane" and thinking that "the unions would go berserk." Men like this suddenly realized why their wives had always wanted to go out on weekends while they had been perfectly happy to just lie around the house. A complete disinterest in sex was another unhappy surprise among this contingent, something they never thought even possible. [26]

Surprisingly, more actively involved dads found parenting less stressful than fathers who spent little time with their kids, a 1983 study found, the latter feeling a considerable degree of guilt about not being there for them. The former also had greater self-esteem and happier marriages, that same study showed, more reason why, in theory at least, men should embrace their role as fathers rather than shun it. [27] This kind of research was good news for social workers trying to address the growing problem of absentee fathers. Teenage pregnancy had long been seen as a serious issue in the United States, especially when the couple was unwed, but historically it had been seen as the mother's predicament. Now there was more consideration of the father's role, with organizations large and small launching programs to help men cope with what was typically a challenging situation. (The number of teenage pregnancies was actually decreasing because of more accessible abortions, but those involved were getting younger and were more likely to keep their babies rather than put them up for adoption.) At the Teenage Pregnancy and Parenting program in San Francisco, for example, young men learned how to change, feed, and hold their babies, skills that were completely alien to those attending the classes. Unlike absentee dads, these fathers wanted to be part of the childcare process but simply did not know how. Similar programs were being offered across the country (most of them funded by the Ford Foundation), a good example of how many men were eager to embrace the joys and responsibilities of fatherhood. Absentee fathers, meanwhile, were growing in numbers, so much so that those concerned about the problem would soon consider it nothing short of a social epidemic. [28]

Those who had experienced "the old fatherhood" were perhaps best qualified to appraise the new one of the 1980s. Having had his first child (a son) in 1958, writer Brock Brower knew firsthand how fatherhood had evolved over the past generation. Brower recalled that fathers of the postwar era had two clear-cut roles—the "provider" and the "decider," the former being firmly based outside the house and the latter inside. Making money at work and serving as "the man of the house," in other words, was what was expected of an American dad. In the early 1960s, however, these sharply defined, easily understood responsibilities began to break down, with the dynamics of fatherhood growing ever fuzzier over the next two decades. (Brower pinpointed the tipping point to have been the publication and popularity of Betty Friedan's 1963 book *The Feminine Mystique*.) "I started helping, not just being, around the house," he recalled in 1984, with four more children (all daughters) to eventually join the family. Besides doing some of the chores that had previously been within his wife's domain, Brower was instrumental in raising his daughters, something he had not been in the first years of his son.[29]

Richard Taylor, a retired philosophy professor, told a similar story a few years later. Taylor, who was sixty-seven years old, had a thirty-nine-year-old son and a one-year-old baby, this almost four decade gap between children allowing him to measure how much fatherhood had changed for him and other older dads. Taylor attended classes prior to his new son's birth and was present when it happened, things he had not experienced back in 1948 for his first child. He was also clueless about basic infant care for his new son, something his much younger wife was surprised by given that he was not a first-time father. For Taylor, the experience of having a baby late in life ran much deeper, however, something quite typical of older fathers (including myself). As a younger man, the professor was heavily invested in his career and social life, but now he was, as he expressed it, "free to focus entirely on my wife and baby." Not having any competing interests, in addition to the wisdom gained from life, were fostering a new and different form of love between he and his baby son (named Aristotle) that Taylor could only describe as "fulfillment." Much had been written about the psychological benefits of receiving pure, unadulterated love from a child but little about the rewards of giving the same kind of love to that child, which was the thing that Taylor found to be such a transformative experience.[30]

As such stories perhaps suggest, the social and cultural ascent of fathers in the 1980s carried with it the idea that men did indeed have some kind of innate paternal instinct. It was almost universally accepted that women had some kind of a maternal instinct, but that men had an equivalent biological drive or impulse to have children was a relatively new idea. Some men, having postponed having kids because they did not want to be tied down, found themselves at around age forty with a strong desire to do so. "It was as if some slow-release time capsule had suddenly gone off in my psyche, unleashing a pool of paternal yearnings," wrote Carey Winfrey, editorial director of CBS Magazines, seeing he and his wife as members of "the growing army of late-blooming urban parents." Warned that having a child in middle age would bring certain difficulties (like not being able to play catch with the little one), Carey had come to the conclusion that the most important requirement for the job was simply the ability to give lots of attention and love. Waiting for the right time was a plus, not a minus, he was sure, feeling he had sufficiently partaken of all other diversions in life.[31]

Ron Hansen also experienced deep paternal yearnings, so much so that he considered there to be a psychological "male clock" not unlike the biological ticking many women felt. Writing for *Esquire* in 1985, Hansen revealed that he became aware of something missing in his midthirties despite an otherwise happy and successful life. As the older generation of his family died off, Hansen sensed an urge to create one of his own, seeing only this as the means to becoming a complete human being. Until that happened, Hansen felt he would remain frozen in time as a young adult wholly dedicated to his career. The ticking was getting louder every year, making him wonder if he would ever have the chance to grow up or, in his words, "have it all." The dangers a child faced every day gave a parent a clear and intense mission in life, something Hansen felt he no longer had. And unlike the women he knew who said they wanted to have a baby, he (and other men in his position) wanted to have a "kid," an important, biologically based distinction. Hansen was looking forward less to his future child's first year than his or her first twenty years, fantasizing about the range of experiences that they could share.[32]

Although many men shared a deep desire to have a child, some made it perfectly clear that they did not want to have another. That was the case for journalist Jerry Adler, who presented his feelings on the subject for *Esquire*. Adler viewed becoming a parent as somewhat of a noble mission, expressing his decision in philosophical terms. "To bring another life into the world represented an affirmation of hope over cynicism, of community over alienation, of joy over despair," he wrote in 1985, seeing the enterprise as nothing less than "a moral act." His wife, however, had no such philosophical foundation to have a baby, at least as Adler saw it; her decision was based on the simpler, more sensual principle that "they feel so good." Given this perspective, it was not surprising that while his wife leaned toward wanting to have another baby, he had no such longing. The first (and, for Adler, hopefully only) child satisfied the moral underpinnings of parenthood, making the prospect of having another more of a burden than anything else. His son was "my own tiny contribution to the forces of life in their never-ending struggle with the legions of death," Adler rather grandiosely expressed it, seeing his philosophical charge as a father now complete.[33]

MARRIED WITH CHILDREN

While some men like Adler defined their role as parents in noble terms, American popular culture was less kind. As Hugh O'Neill observed in *Parents*, Hollywood had historically not presented fathers as heroes, a reflection perhaps of their relatively low social status in real life. One would never find movie stars like Cary Grant, Humphrey Bogart, John Wayne, or Clint Eastwood buckling a child's seatbelt, driving the baby-sitter home, or mashing up carrots in their films, as such routine paternal activities would never be seen as remotely heroic or even mildly interesting.[34]

Over the past few years, however, Hollywood had in fact injected a good dose of heroism into the makeup of some lead characters. The 1979 movie *Kramer vs. Kramer* marked a turning point in male identity in film, with Dustin Hoffman's character personifying the qualities of the new fatherhood. (The 1978 novel and 1982 film *The World According to Garp* also exemplified the positive values of devoted fatherhood.)[35] In its portrayal of fathers in the 1980s, Hollywood had in some films continued in the tradition of *Kramer vs. Kramer*, presenting men as actively involved with if not completely devoted to their children. Movies such as *Ordinary People* (1980), *On Golden Pond* (1981), and *Tender Mercies* (1983) depicted fathers as flawed yet loving characters, a reversal of the parentally distracted cinematic dads of the late 1960s and 1970s. Less popular films like *Tribute* (1980), *Author! Author!* (1982), *Six Weeks* (1982), *Table for Five* (1983), and *Man, Woman and Child* (1983) also fell into this category. What had changed? Film critic

Molly Haskell theorized that Hollywood producers, directors, and screenwriters were working out their guilt as workaholics and, more often than not, divorced men, in these emotion-laden, male-driven movies. By choosing to make such films, moguls might have also been expressing anger at their own bottled-up or inattentive fathers, Haskell suggested. Old wrongs were typically righted or some kind of retribution earned in the genre, she pointed out, with custody of children not automatically awarded to mothers. (Men were actually winning more than their share of such court battles in real life.) Haskell referred to these movies as "father-child valentines" and "paean[s] to the emotional and domestic virtuosity of the male," taking a swipe with the industry's depiction of women.[36]

While Hollywood had suddenly discovered heroism in simply being a father, television shows of the 1980s reinforced the image of the superdad in the public's imagination. In prime-time soaps such as *Dallas*, *Dynasty*, *Knot's Landing*, *Falcon Crest*, and *The Colbys*, wealthy patriarchs used their money and power to perpetuate the family's legacy (often with disappointing results). *The Cosby Show*, however, was the very model of proper parenting, with the lead character humorously demonstrating both the joys and frustrations in being a modern-day dad. Things were more problematic in shows like *Rosanne*, *thirtysomething*, and *The Wonder Years*, each of these portraying the tensions of family life with more realism. (*Married with Children*, on the other hand, turned them into genuine, if less than tasteful, farce.) Stay-at-home dads were featured in both *Growing Pains* and *Who's the Boss?*, these mainstream sitcoms proof that fathers, upon returning from work, no longer had to greet their wives with "Honey, I'm home!"

If there was one seminal event within the universe of popular culture related to fatherhood in the 1980s, a very good case could be made that it was the publication of Bill Cosby's book *Fatherhood*. The 1986 book sent fatherhood (and the publishing business) on a new trajectory, the beginnings of a new literary genre devoted to personal stories of parenting. Cosby's book (which was at least partly written by humorist Ralph Schoenstein) injected humor and celebrity into the usually serious subject of fatherhood, nicely countering the high-charging, overly earnest "superdad." In real life, Cosby and his wife Camille had five children aged nine to twenty-one at the time (Erika, Erinn, Ensa, Ervin, and Ennis, the latter murdered in 1997), ideal qualifications to reflect on the joys and challenges of fatherhood and the effect it had on marriage. His wife and children were actually never mentioned by name in the book, but given the keenly observant stories told, they had no need to be.

Published precisely in the right place and at the right time, *Fatherhood* immediately became a cultural phenomenon. In his book, the forty-eight-year-old Cosby illustrated a lighter side of parenting as no one had previously done, which resonated strongly with readers. Cosby borrowed freely from both his stand-up monologue and television show in putting together the anecdotes for *Fatherhood*, something that no doubt contributed heavily to it becoming not just a bestseller but one of the blockbusters of the year and decade. The comedian's titular show was extremely highly rated when the book was released, giving him a promotional platform that was perhaps unprecedented in literary history. The show, which ran for eight seasons and aired almost two hundred episodes, still ranks as one of the most popular sitcoms ever broadcast. Americans had not tuned into a home-based sitcom in such numbers since *I Love Lucy*, making some wonder what was behind the phenomenon that was *The Cosby Show*. "We missed the TV dad, missed his authority and were waiting for his return," explained Peter W. Kaplan in *Esquire*, seeing the Cliff Huxtable character as a televisual descendent of Ozzie Nelson of *Ozzie and Harriet*, Jim Anderson of *Father Knows Best*, Danny Thomas of *Make Room for Daddy*, Steve Douglas of *My Three Sons*, Ward Cleaver of *Leave It to Beaver*, and Rob Petrie of *The Dick Van Dyke Show*. Cosby's character "has everything the old dads had, but he's more powerful, more authoritative, more outraged," continued Kaplan, considering Huxtable to be "the highest synthesis of TV fatherhood four decades in the making."[37]

Given the ubiquity and seeming reality of *The Cosby Show*, it was difficult to tell where the fiction of the television show ended and the nonfiction of *Fatherhood* began. In each, fatherhood had none of the professed nobility Adler had assigned to it or any of Hollywood's heroism. More simply, being a dad was presented as a dimension of life that was worth undertaking even with all of its craziness and trouble. While obviously loving his kids and being a father, Cosby was unafraid to take jabs at the loony situations in which any dad found himself on a regular basis. The book served as a parental advice book without ever saying so, offering readers useful tips on what to do and what not to do when treading the often choppy waters of fatherhood. The man was not afraid to admit he was flummoxed when it came to being an American dad, speaking of the subject honestly and candidly rather than as a know-it-all expert. "Child raising is still a dark continent and no one really knows anything," he confessed, describing being a father as "sweet insanity." Cosby also talked about how having kids changed him and his wife, a refreshing, all-too-rare perspective in the voluminous body of literature dedicated to parenting. As well, the rich and famous comedian was frequently self-deprecating, confessing that he was hardly the king of the castle in which he dwelled. Readers obviously related to the book, finding they had much in common with the man, at least when it came to being a father.[38]

Cosby somehow found the time for both his demanding career and his busy home life, but others were not so lucky. Many dads were struggling mightily with having to burn the candle at both ends, finding that being both a good father and a good employee was difficult if not impossible. Men were pulling off rather amazing juggling acts just to get through a normal day, wondering how much longer they could keep the balls in the air. Things were not easy at all for those in the lower middle and working classes, as the social and economic gap between the haves and have-nots widened in the 1980s.[39] Even relatively well-off young urban professionals with kids felt the pressure, not at all sure they could fulfill their ambitious career goals and be the great dads they had every intention of being. Most companies in the mid-1980s were less than understanding when managers asked their bosses for occasional flextime. Some responded by offering the stressed-out employee a bigger title and higher salary, not at all what he had requested. The simple fact was that high-profile jobs were usually not just nine to five but involved evenings and weekends, a recipe for disaster if one expected to spend time with the kids (and the wife). Women too were increasingly pursuing busy careers while raising kids, these supermoms also trying to have it all.[40] As with supermoms, the male equivalent was attempting to squeeze more into a day than humanly possible. "Like their busy wives," *Newsweek* wrote in 1986, "this small but growing army of would-be superdads is experiencing not only the joys of parenthood but also the frustrations of trying to combine work and family."[41] Divorces were on the rise, not surprisingly, as both mothers and fathers painfully came to the conclusion that they did not possess superpowers.

Seemingly the happiest of marriages were those in which each partner was able to strike a balance among parenting, work, and some kind
of social life. "Balance is fast becoming a buzzword among baby boomers," noted *Fortune* in 1988, the pressures to be both a good employee
and good parent making that desired state difficult to achieve. Some
managers found themselves delegating more than they otherwise
would, allowing them to spend time with their kids mornings, evenings,
and weekends. Economists and sociologists were intrigued by the new,
growing class of "dual-career couples," having never seen such a group
before, at least in significant numbers. Traditional gender roles appeared to have little or no value to many young, married executives, nor
did the notion of limits. What Yale psychiatrist Daniel Levinson called
in his book *The Seasons of a Man's Life* the "Big Bang" typically upset
the delicate balance of dual-career couples; the arrival of a baby
wreaked havoc with the partners' busy schedules. While women had
struggled with managing parenthood and careers for a couple of
decades at this point, doing the same was a relatively new thing for this
generation of men. New fathers who never would have thought of going
to a psychologist were doing so, finding their definition of success in the
workplace and being a near-perfect parent and husband mutually exclusive. Men were gradually realizing they had to lower expectations and
make choices, not an easy thing to do for baby boomers trained in the
ethos that anything and everything was possible. [42]

If not called "superdads," men who found themselves juggling careers and parenthood were sometimes called "working fathers." Like
"working mothers," from which the term derived, working fathers
found themselves having to walk a fine line between home and employer. "Functioning as the primary breadwinner while competing in a corporate environment that undervalues and even punishes caring fathers
has created unfamiliar problems and pressures for men," noted *U.S.
News & World Report* in 1988. Many companies were just getting used
to women taking time off or working flextime because of kids, making
male employees' request for such unwelcome news. "Why the need for
paternity leave if moms were staying home to take care of a newborn?"
some human resources managers wondered, ironically applying a double standard for men. As recently as the mid-1980s, childcare was considered a female issue, but now, just a few years later, it had become a
priority for men as well. With the 1987 stock market crash, the eighties

boom had gone bust, making men all the more reluctant to broach the subject with their bosses (and sometimes their wives). But more companies were doing what they could to accommodate the schedules of "working fathers," seeing that as a way to keep talented employees from going to a competitor. Corporate daycare was one innovative solution to the problem, with some companies like Domino's Pizza actually allowing fathers to watch over their kids while working in their office once a week.[43]

Even if one had no intention to be a "superdad," there was significant pressure for men to embrace the values and lifestyle of "the new fatherhood." Fathers who did not know what they were getting into when they had a child five, ten, or fifteen years earlier found themselves in a difficult spot, feeling both their wives and bosses were less than pleased with how they were managing their time. While some dads eagerly seized the opportunities to be had with eighties-style fatherhood, others believed they had it thrust upon them. "Most fathers have become reluctant warriors in a social revolution," *Newsweek* reported, their more active role in parenting not sought after but rather assigned to them. Many wives had only recently taken full-time jobs, leaving men with more childcare and housework responsibilities, and the new expectations to be sensitive and nurturing people was for some a foreign concept. But the more time fathers, reluctant or otherwise, spent with their young children, the more they tended to enjoy the experience. "Over time, the child worm[s] its way into the emotional life of the father, ma[kes] the father feel valued," Yale psychologist Kyle Pruett found in his research, finding that it was "these men [who] became real father junkies."[44]

A DOUBLE BIND

American dads who fully embraced the joys and challenges of fatherhood did so despite the lingering social bias against them. Jerrold Lee Shapiro, a professor at the University of Santa Clara and family therapist, experienced this firsthand after he and his wife had a child. "To the proud parents, especially the mother, who did all the work," read a congratulatory card from Shapiro's family, rubbing him the wrong way. Although the message was clearly tongue-in-cheek, Shapiro felt it symbolized the true sentiment held toward parenting and, particularly, fathers. While motherhood and mothers were cherished, as they should be, fatherhood and fathers were not, an unfair and unfortunate state of affairs given men's central role in the creation and raising of children. Men did not bear children, of course, but in some emotional and psychological ways they were invested just as much in the parenting process, Shapiro believed, something not generally recognized. Expectations for fathers were now high, but with no role models to follow, men were essentially blazing uncharted territory.[45]

Given the cultural favoritism shown to mothers, fathers were simultaneously inside and outside the parental unit, one could fairly say, not an easy place to be. Fathers were expected to play an active role in parenting, but few people were truly interested in how they felt about it, especially if those feelings involved anxiety, anger, sadness, or fear. (Surveys showed that it was quite common for new fathers to feel significant pressure in having to provide for the family. The fear that one or one's spouse might die was another major concern among first-time dads, something life insurance salesmen knew all too well.) Mothers-to-be and first-time mothers were naturally predisposed toward all sorts of emotions, everyone knew, but this was not considered the case for fathers-to-be or first-time fathers. "He's caught in a double bind," Shapiro summed up fathers' situation in *Psychology Today* in 1987, their presence insisted upon as long as they did not share any "negative" emotions about the complicated experience of being a dad.[46]

For all the talk about the "superdad" or "Mr. Mom," however, there were in fact few men who legitimately fell into either category. (The same could have been said for "yuppies," who despite the media frenzy surrounding them, comprised just about 5 percent of the population.)[47] Some experts held that the "Mr. Mom" phenomenon (named after the 1983 movie in which a breadwinning father and stay-at-home mother swap roles after the former loses his job) was largely a myth; social observers, they insisted, were pushing the characteristics of the new fatherhood too far. Studies indeed showed that men still fell well short of women when it came to both childcare and housework, and that the former tended to select the less laborious jobs when dividing up the domestic pie. Young fathers in the 1980s grew up in the sixties, that is, before the women's liberation movement, something that likely encouraged them to cling to traditional gender roles despite the "social revolution" currently playing out. [48]

More revolutionary, perhaps, were parental changes taking place within the legal sphere. Some fathers were going to court to prevent women from having abortions, something men had failed to do a dozen years earlier when the Supreme Court ruled against that right. A new court was in place in the late 1980s (conservative Justice Anthony Kennedy had replaced more liberal Justice Lewis F. Powell), however, giving pro-life activists hope that the decision would be reversed. (Overturning *Roe v. Wade* was this contingent's ultimate goal.) Should fathers have some say over whether the fetus they had co-conceived was born, or was it strictly the mother's decision? The answer was not clear, particularly as fathers' status as parents escalated through the 1980s. [49]

Fathers who did not pay child support represented another legal issue getting more attention in the late 1980s. Around 5.6 million Americans under age fifteen lived in fatherless homes, and only a third of them received financial support from their biological dads. Going to court to make the "deadbeat dads" pay up was often futile, leaving many of the kids in poverty. (Some fathers withheld their payments as retaliation for their ex-partner's not granting them court-ordered visitation rights.) Recognizing a bigger stick was needed, Congress stepped in by including in its welfare reform bill a provision that would allow states to take out the required payments from paychecks. Should that not work for some reason, more deadbeat dads would be headed for jail, which would not solve the problem but perhaps act as an incentive for other noncustodial parents to pony up. [50]

Had they been aware of the emotional benefits to be realized from fatherhood, more deadbeat dads might have chosen to be involved in their kids' lives, whatever the cost. A then recently published longitudinal study of more than two hundred fathers revealed that being a dad was a positive experience in a psychological sense, functioning as a means of developing greater empathy and compassion. (The finding was consistent with Erik Erikson's theory of "generativity," which held that humans achieved full maturity only when they advanced the lives of children in some way.) The other good news in this study was that, contrary to popular belief, the careers of men did not suffer when they became fathers or stepped up their involvement; any missed opportunity or slowdown in completing a project proved to be only temporary.

And, as previous studies showed, children benefited greatly from having their dad around. Both boys and girls became more confident, mature, and autonomous adults with the presence of an engaged father, the study by psychologists Joseph Pleck, John Snarey, and Anthony Maier found, with the authors declaring fatherhood a clear win-win experience. "The role of the father is just as important as the role of the mother," Snarey stated, something many dads likely suspected but were still happy to hear.[51]

In fact, one could go as far as to say that fathers were "superior" to mothers in some aspects of child raising. Research showed that toddlers were more compliant with their dads and were more likely to follow rules they had set. The reasons for this were unclear. One theory was that fathers simply spent less time with their kids, making the latter appreciate the time they did spend with them; another was the even simpler explanation that men typically had a more commanding voice and physical presence than women. As any parent well knows, young children quickly became very good at playing mom and dad like fiddles. "She senses, and predicts, how each of you reacts to her and to what she does, and she is learning how to make that knowledge work for her," wrote Bernice Weissbourd in *Parents* in 1989. Weissbourd, who was head of a childcare center in Chicago, went further by emphasizing that children had different and separate relationships with their mothers and fathers, something often overlooked in all the discourse about parenting.[52]

Given more credit for what they brought to the parental party, American dads were experiencing a cultural zenith of sorts as the eighties ended. Regardless of how many dads actually qualified, "the new fatherhood" had become the dominant expression of paternity, raising the social status of men in general. For decades, fathers were considered second-class citizens when it came to parenting, but now they were seen as having a shared partnership with mothers, a major transformation in both gender identity and family dynamics. "It's official—fathers are no longer the invisible parent," exclaimed Roger M. Barkin in 1989, with the sociological changes bringing not only greater opportunities for male parents but bigger challenges as well. Barkin, chair of pediatrics at Rose Medical Center in Denver and the author of *The Father's Guide*, believed that the myth that men were ill equipped for raising children had finally been debunked. Historically considered good providers and disciplinarians but poor nurturers, fathers had been redeemed, one could say, their image much improved over the course of just one generation. "Bringing home a paycheck and periodically reading an obligatory bedtime story is not the model for today's fathers," he continued, the range of dads' responsibilities dramatically expanded.[53]

Indeed, expressions of the new fatherhood could be detected in real, observable ways. Twenty-five percent of fathers in the early 1970s were in the delivery room when their baby was born while over 75 percent were in the late 1980s—just one example of how dads' parental presence had literally increased. Feeding and changing babies had not that long ago been largely alien tasks for fathers, but now they were common, this too helping to reconstruct the makeup of masculinity in the United States. The recently developed partnership between mothers and fathers had benefits beyond its egalitarianism. Relationships between spouses and with children were said to improve when there was more of a parental balance, and kids were believed to more easily establish friendships with their peers. As well, new or strange situations were less troublesome for kids who had grown up in homes where both mothers and fathers had substantially contributed to the parenting process, experts held, more ammunition for a dualistic approach to child raising.[54]

While the new fatherhood was broadly viewed as better than "the old fatherhood" in many respects, some argued that there remained significant strides for men to take if they were to realize their full potential as parents. Fathers were still often seen as having a minority stake in parenting, with mothers clearly in charge of the operation. Men had to be coaxed into taking part in childcare, the traditional view went, an idea that was not even considered for women. In 1989, for example, *Parents* urged wives to "help [their] husband be a great dad," advice made even more peculiar given that it was presented as something in the best interests of new mothers rather than new fathers. "If you are smart," the magazine told women, "you will do everything you can during the first few months after your baby's birth to encourage your husband to be a father who takes pride in helping." Moms would be happier if such a thing was achieved, *Parents* felt, with no real thought given to how dads would feel by "helping." Instead of being seen as an equal partner in the joint venture of parenting, fathers were thus portrayed as junior assistants who required direction and supervision, a distinctly postwar point of view.[55] Another 1989 article in *Parents* sent the message that even "superdads" were mere mortals. Dad was "doing more," the magazine conceded, "but mom still calls the shots."[56]

Such quibbling aside, there was little argument that the American dad had been reinvented over the past generation or two. In a special guide for fathers and fathers-to-be published in 1989, *Esquire* proposed that three factors accounted for the dramatic changes in fatherhood over the past three or four decades. It was information, feminism, and therapy that transformed the postwar father into the American dad of the late 1980s, the editors of the magazine argued, an obviously simplistic yet not entirely unreasonable thesis. Regarding information, fathers of the 1950s relied heavily on the parental advice of one man—Dr. Spock—while now there was a whole section of resources at bookstores for dads looking for some guidance. (The Internet would soon exponentially multiply the amount of information for parents.) Hundreds of parenting books were being published annually, making it almost inexcusable for any father not to be familiar with the basic principles of childcare. The second major factor, feminism, not only gave men greater childcare responsibilities but did much to lessen gender stereotyping of both boys and girls, the *Esquire* article continued. Finally, the therapeutic culture of the last few decades provided many fathers with a psychological portrait of their childhood, something they applied in the raising of their own kids.[57]

While certainly important and, perhaps, revolutionary, many of the pursuits of "the new fatherhood" could be seen as simple replications of motherhood. Men were being applauded for taking on some of the responsibilities of women, a domestic version of the increasing gender equality occurring in the workplace. Sustainable change relied on both men and women adopting a parenting style that was true to and consistent with their gender, something that had yet to be achieved. As the nation entered the final decade of the twentieth century, however, such a change would take hold, and the American dad would be reborn yet again.

3

THE DADDYTRACK

Fatherhood is hot right now.

—Judith Davidoff, 1999

Anyone seeing an advertisement in a magazine or a commercial on television in 1990 might have been taken aback when coming across an image of a man. For the past decade, the Gordon Gekko–like power-broker and preppy Yuppie had each served as iconic representations of male identity in popular and consumer culture. Now, however, men were increasingly portrayed as fathers in advertising, a reflection of the major cultural shift that was taking place in America. In ads and commercials, men had discarded their power suits, briefcases, and running shoes and had accumulated, of all things, children. "The ultimate hero of the '90s will be the best dad," explained advertising executive Mal MacDougall, believing the terms of what comprised success had recently and dramatically changed. Michael Jordan and the Marlboro Man remained visible symbols of machismo, but big-name marketers like Oreo and the Gap were featuring fathers and children in their advertising, conveying a softer, more sensitive side of masculinity that seemed new and different.[1]

Mr. MacDougall's prediction would turn out to be correct. The reinvention of masculinity in advertising was part of something bigger, as what would come to be known as "the fatherhood movement" infiltrated the cultural zeitgeist at the end of the twentieth century. Fatherhood, both the idea and the practice, realized a higher degree of social currency in the 1990s as the nation turned away from the materialism and excesses of the previous decade. Many men were eager to get on what many referred to as the "daddytrack," a course that promised true and deep meaning and purpose in life. Baby boomers' settling down and having kids was a big part of this, as was the growing number of studies indicating the importance of fathers within the family. Conservatives linked the absence of dads to all kinds of serious social ills, this too elevating the cultural status of fatherhood. Political leaders and celebrities seized on the new interest in and concern over fatherhood, the once simple state of paternity now in vogue. And if it were not clear enough, fathers were not at all the same as mothers, with children the beneficiaries of a two-pronged approach to parenting. The American dad was much more than "Mr. Mom," many were coming to believe, as a new kind of masculine identity was forged.

THE SLY FOX

Anyone taking a long view could see the vast changes that had taken place in family life and gender roles in the United States. Writing for *Parents* in 1990, Katherine Karlsrud and Dodi Schultz observed that American dads had made great strides since the 1950s, when Jim Anderson of the popular television show *Father Knows Best* served as the model of fatherhood. Then limited to making money and disciplining children when necessary, fathers expanded their role in family matters immensely in the 1970s and 1980s, assuming a much more active role in childcare. Now many fathers showed no hesitancy in changing diapers or fixing their daughters' hair, leveling the parental field. Still, dads had some way to go, Karlsrud, a New York City pediatrician, and Schultz, coauthor of *The First Five Years*, felt, thinking that significant numbers of fathers were not completely comfortable taking care of their babies. "It seems to me that the desire to be involved is there," they suggested, "but there's a certain amount of hesitancy or awkwardness." Fathers were reluctant to bring their little ones in for a checkup, Karlsrud noted, and some had little idea how to undress them in her office. Today's dads still had some Jim Anderson left in them, the two posited, a remnant of their own fathers' lack of experience with very young children. "If parents are to play an equal role, fathers need to become actively involved in caring for the baby," they concluded, believing a truly fair expression of parenthood had yet to be achieved in the United States.[2]

Some fathers, however, resented what they saw as men's second-class status as parents. Society discriminated against men because of lingering gender identities, Erik Larson felt, citing some of his own, rather upsetting experiences as a dad. "Playing Mommy today?" asked one of his neighbors upon seeing him play with his daughter outside, as if it were unusual that "Daddy" was spending time with his kid. (As a writer, Larson had a more flexible schedule than his wife, who worked in a hospital.) Attending a parent-teacher meeting with his wife was similarly discouraging, as the teachers spoke only to Larson's wife as if he was not even there. Doctors too treated Larson as what he described as a "go-between," someone responsible for just relaying information from and to his wife. One man with whom Larson spoke reported that women he did not even know occasionally stopped him to say what a good job he was doing with his two sons. Would a mother be told anything like this? Larson wondered. Unlikely, he felt, describing the man's story as a kind of reverse chauvinism. Besides being simply annoying, such experiences had a subtle but real effect on how parents parented, Larson believed, pushing moms and dads into adopting more traditional gender roles.[3]

Still, there was little doubt that this generation of fathers received a good degree more respect than did the last. The changes brought forth by the "superdad" of the 1980s were still resonating strongly in the early 1990s, laying the foundation for whatever would come next. In 1992, *Parents* humorously compared the current state of fatherhood with that of the previous generation, illustrating the degree to which the role of dads had been transformed. Dads of the postwar years probably never baked cookies with their children, for example, or hung their artwork in their office. A father staying home from work with a sick child was not probable back then, nor would he have been likely to take that sniffling toddler to the pediatrician. The list of new domestic and familial responsibilities contemporary dads had went on and on, from diapering to cleaning the house to doing laundry to shopping. As well, fathers of the day were telling their kids touchy-feely things like "Share your feelings" or "It's okay to cry," parental advice that would not have been in their own dads' repertoire. Relationships with sons and daughters had deepened and become much more personal, with the clear gender lines of the Eisenhower era now almost indistinguishable. There was no doubt that fatherhood had, over the course of one generation, been turned into something much different and more complicated.[4]

Best of all, perhaps, "the new fatherhood" appeared to cross the lines of social and economic class as well as those of race. Backed up by some research studies, it was commonly believed that this different kind of involved dad was typically upper middle class and held a professional job. But many working-class men were spending lots of quality time with their children, new studies showed, a sign that this brand of parenting had become deeply entrenched in American society. "As many as 44% of America's dads are hurling themselves into the engaging, messy mayhem of their children's daily lives," reported Lisa Schroepfer in *American Health* in 1991, with "real men" rather than just the cultural elite joining the cause. Blue-collar types wanted to actively shape their kids' lives just as much as doctors and lawyers, according to the latest research, with equal recognition that doing so could be the most gratifying thing in the world. The need for two paychecks was another factor for lower-middle-class fathers to commit to a heavy load of childcare, as it was likely that moms also held a full-time job (or a couple of part-times). Importantly, children benefited from two active parents, the studies also indicated, with a combination of styles likely to build self-confidence, instill empathy, and foster happiness in either a son or a daughter.[5]

Popular culture, particularly children's literature, however, had yet to catch up to the big changes in fatherhood. Upon reading one of his two-year-old daughter's favorite books, *Mother Goose and the Sly Fox*, Armin Brott, a freelance writer, was surprised by how different the mother and father were depicted. The mom (Mother Goose) was a wonderful caretaker for her little ones (and ran a successful lace business on the side), while the dad (the Fox) was shown to be, as Brott put it, "a neglectful and presumably unemployed single father [who] lives with his filthy, hungry pups in a grimy hovel." Thinking he may be onto something, Brott did yeoman's work by plopping down in the children's book area of his local library in Berkeley, California, and reading dozens of stories. His conclusion? "The majority of children's classics perpetuate negative male stereotypes," he wrote for *Newsweek* in 1992, with mothers typically presented as the primary caregivers and fathers, if included at all, finding little time to spend with children.[6] Brott's piece received a lot of attention, and over the next decade he was able to leverage his fathers-get-no-respect platform into no less than five books about fatherhood: *The Expectant Father, The New Father*, and *Fathering Your Toddler, Throwaway Dads*, and *The Single Father*.

Dads on early 1990s television, meanwhile, erred on the side of being too involved and benevolent. Cliff Huxtable, Bill Cosby's role on *The Cosby Show*, was an obstetrician who seemed to have an inordinate amount of time to spend with his five precocious but well-meaning kids. And when he did get upset at one of his teenagers, his anger was brief and humorous, something that could not be said for many real-life fathers of teens. Likewise, the Michael Steadman character on *thirty-something* was equally nice and congenial, even when he caught a baby-sitter spending time with her boyfriend rather than his three-year-old. "Cliff Huxtable and Michael Steadman are so revoltingly kind, patient, and understanding that they make Dr. Spock seem like Attila the Hun," joked David S. Machlowitz in *Parents*, calling the characters "perfect-angel" fathers who bore little resemblance to any dads he knew (including himself). The other paternal archetype on television was the "perfect-nincompoop" who played the foil (or fool) of their respective show. (Dads had played this role since the early days of television and, before that, radio.) The fathers in *Major Dad, Growing Pains*, and *The Hogan Family* all fell into this category, Machlowitz believed, feeling television would be well served by a couple of genuine, competent dads.[7]

Hollywood too had caught the fatherhood bug but resisted portraying dads as crafty ne'er-do-wells, perfect role models, or simpletons. As in advertising, men had recently been recast in movies, with fathers often placed squarely in the center of plot points. "The most interesting resurrection of the cinematic male soul in recent months is to be found in the dozen or so films about fathers, or father-figures," wrote Elayne Rapping in the *Progressive* in November 1993, considering fatherhood to be "a real growth industry in Hollywood." Rather suddenly, men's parenting skills (or lack thereof) were the focus of a fair number of mainstream movies, with a parallel shift from what had been the common arenas of masculinity (business and war, principally) to domestic matters. Rapping cited a slew of recently released films—*The Man Without a Face, Sleepless in Seattle, Jurassic Park, Searching for Bobby Fischer, This Boy's Life, King of the Hill, Jack the Bear, American Heart, A Far Off Place, A River Runs Through It, Dennis the Menace,*

Last Action Hero, and *The Adventures of Huck Finn*—in which father-hood or the counseling of kids was the primary theme. Interestingly (and disturbingly), all but one (*Jurassic Park*) of the films featured a boy as the child to be mentored, a throwback of sorts to the 1950s when daughters were difficult to find in narratives of fatherhood. The arc of these movies was routine and predictable, as Rapping noted, with the less-than-heroic lead character fully redeeming himself by the closing credits. "A man totally uninterested and unfit for fatherhood goes through a change of character in which he learns to care for and about a young boy and bond with him," she described the storyline, thinking that some of the films "could serve as instructional tracts for prospective fathers."[8] The 1994 *Getting Even with Dad* was another paternal re-demption story that glorified fatherhood. In the movie, Ted Danson plays an ex-con and widower and Macaulay Culkin the son he has effec-tively abandoned. By film's end, however, the two are reunited, as Dan-son's character comes to understand that being a good father is more rewarding than even a lucrative heist.

Although it was a classic Hollywood trope, a man's journey to achieve a higher level of being through fatherhood was believed by experts to have much truth in real life. "We know that being a father is life's fullest expression of masculinity," wrote Frank Pittman in his 1993 book *Man Enough*, wondering why so many men had historically failed to recognize this. Pittman, a physician, did not hold back in describing the value of fatherhood, seeing it as "the central experience of life, the greatest source of self-awareness, the true fountain of pride and joy, [and] the most eternal bond with a partner." Like others falling on the more conservative side of the fence, Pittman believed being a dad was "what it takes to be a man," the ultimate role he should play in life. The workings of capitalism had thrown men off their natural course, he suggested in his book, the reason why masculinity had since the Indus-trial Revolution been primarily defined by money and success. Chil-dren, especially sons, hungered for their "lost fathers," his rather elab-orate theory continued, with all sorts of negative actions including crim-inal behavior, a lack of ethics in the business world, and cheating on one's spouse the sad result. Now, however, there was "a new generation of nurturers," making Pittman optimistic that the children of the future would grow up to be more emotionally secure and, ultimately, better dads.[9]

Fred Barnes, a columnist for the *New Republic*, had a much different view of the situation. "Fatherhood isn't brain surgery," he believed, thinking the big fuss currently being made about it was much ado about nothing. Most men had a natural instinct for being good dads, he held, with no social movement needed to get them to embrace fatherhood. If 90 percent of life was just showing up, as Woody Allen had quipped, 90 percent of fatherhood was simply being there, Barnes argued, a refreshing, contrarian attitude explaining men's headlong rush to get on the "daddytrack." And rather than "quality time" it was "quantity time" that really mattered, he suggested; his views were shaped heavily by his own experience with his four kids, who "crave[d] prolonged attention, preferably undivided."[10] Ben Stein, the actor/writer/commentator, agreed. "The key to a happy child is having a dad who is there with him [or her] consistently, day in and day out," the genius explained, thinking this not-very-glamorous brand of fatherhood was far superior to that of the more flashy "Saturday afternoon dad." Rather than buying toys for a child or taking him or her to a movie—exactly what many workaholics did to appease their guilt—it was "knowing that Dad is always there for him [or her]" that was important, Stein held, he too lobbying for quantity over quality.[11]

No one had to tell that to Sean Elder, a self-described "all-day dad" who occasionally found the time to write a freelance article. With his wife bringing home the bacon, Elder bore the principal responsibilities of raising their toddler, Franny, something that distinguished him and other all-day dads from those he called "Gentlemen Fathers." Much like the "Saturday afternoon dad," "Gentleman Fathers" held full-time jobs and dabbled in childcare, by itself nothing to be ashamed of. But gentleman fathers took an unusual amount of pride—too much in fact—for the contributions they did decide to make. Like gentlemen farmers, gentleman fathers were in it more for fun than anything else, a very different story than "professionals" like himself. "Mine is the full-throttle, sunrise-to-sunset experience most dads never know, though some pretend to," Elder wrote in the *New York Times* in 1995, making a clear distinction between this brand of fatherhood and the other, more common variety that was not unlike a hobby.[12]

A LONG WAY TO GO

Pittman may have gone a bit too far in his analysis of fatherhood in America and Barnes not far enough, but the consensus was that a page had indeed been turned in recent years. "Men may still have a long way to go," noted Richard Louv in *Parents* in 1993, "but in its slow and steady way, fatherhood in America is moving toward maturity." Louv was basing his opinion on the results of a survey the magazine had taken of some 8,200 men. The last such poll the magazine had conducted was a decade earlier, so a comparison between the state of fatherhood in the early 1980s and early 1990s could be made. Fathers had almost "caught up" with mothers in nearly all aspects of childcare over this ten-year stretch of time, good news for those believing that gender parity at home was a positive thing. The most telling insights from the survey, however, could be found in the individual comments made about being a dad. "I feel more human, more alive, more of everything," said one father from Rockport, Massachusetts; another from Stockton, California, asked, "Is it worth it?" answering his own question, "Unequivocal[ly] yes!"[13]

Interestingly, part of the reported "aliveness" of new fathers was the considerable anxiety associated with having to constantly look out for a child, echoing the thoughts of many if not most dads. ("Without a doubt, the most terrifying and fulfilling part of my life is being a father," Robert J. Samuelson of *Newsweek* wrote a few years later, nicely capturing the bipolar rollercoaster ride that was fatherhood.)[14] *Parents* also decided to include a curious question in its survey: Which actor would "play you in a movie about your life as a father?" The respondents' top choices were fairly predictable—Kevin Costner, Tim Allen, and Tom Hanks—all actors who usually played nice guys in films and appeared to be nice guys in real life. Seventh on the list was Jimmy Stewart, however, somewhat odd considering that the legendary actor was then eighty-five years old and had not made a feature film in a couple of decades.[15]

Although the media were clearly taken with the idea that there was a "new fatherhood," one did not have to be an expert to notice that the concept was very much like what could be called "the old motherhood." American dads were now expected to have a strong nurturing instinct and share homemaking activities, preferably on an equal basis with their wives if the latter also worked. Just as the playing field had been significantly leveled in the workplace, it appeared that the one on the domestic front had equivalently flattened out across gender lines. This parallel development was hardly a coincidence, of course; each shift was a product of the call for greater equality in all aspects of life. Was all this "social androgyny" a positive thing, some wondered? More extreme conservatives believed that fairness in the workplace was all well and good, but that the erosion of traditional gender roles at home was not healthy for marriages or child raising. Men and women were, biologically at least, different, they argued, and pretending they were not could be a dangerous thing.[16]

The ideological divide over the role of men in the family reflected the general fuzziness of fatherhood in the early 1990s. "Fatherhood has lost its cultural coherence," said Robert Griswold in 1993, with no clear agreement on the degree to which or how American dads should contribute to child raising. Griswold, an associate professor of history and women's studies at the University of Oklahoma, was getting a lot of attention with his new book *Fatherhood in America*, in which he convincingly showed that the subject was, historically speaking, a work in progress. In his book, Griswold took readers through the transformation of fatherhood that took place between the world wars, when dads established a closer and, specifically, friendlier relationship with their children (especially boys). "The opinion was that fathers needed to be, in a sense, a buddy," he observed, a role that demanded little of the necessary heavy lifting that went into raising children. It was not until the 1970s and 1980s that fathers took on a significant share of child raising and domestic responsibilities, however, as the feminist movement and rise of the "working woman" recast the attitudes and behavior of men. Now, in the 1990s, parenting was what Griswold called a "negotiable enterprise," with virtually all family matters up for grabs.[17]

With parenthood now firmly seen as a collaborative or joint venture, part of being a good dad was the expectation to be directly involved in the mother's pregnancy. Taking care of the baby thus extended well before it was actually born, with special attention to be paid to moms, who were obviously bearing the brunt of the burden. Preparing for the birth itself was particularly important, with men urged to do whatever they could to make the mother comfortable and, as Sheldon H. Cherry put it, "share the pregnancy experience." Men should go with their partners to doctor appointments, experts advised, and make a point of hearing the fetal heartbeat together for the first time. Like most physicians, Cherry, a clinical professor of obstetrics and gynecology at Mount Sinai Hospital in New York, recommended that men attend childbirth-preparation classes together with their partners as a good way to feel involved.[18] Classes in Lamaze, the natural childbirth technique developed in the 1940s, remained popular in the 1990s, in part because it gave fathers an important role during their partner's pregnancy and in the delivery process. In Lamaze, men were not just observers but "coaches," an essential part of the birthing team. Through Lamaze and other team-based birthing techniques, men were being trained to be supportive partners to mothers and to be good fathers by bonding with the baby-to-be.

Regardless of the delivery technique, fathers were expected to play an important, coachlike role in childbirth. "He'll expect to call at least some of the plays from the sidelines," wrote Fay Stevenson-Smith and Dena K. Salmon in *Parents* in 1993, continuing the sports metaphor to perhaps appeal to men. Childbirth classes were certainly helpful, not unlike a team's practice sessions, but it was game day where the true stars would stand out. "Coping with real labor can be quite different," Stevenson-Smith, an obstetrician, and Salmon, a freelance writer, admitted, the sights and sounds of delivery capable of reducing the manliest of men to a blubbering mess. (It was the job of mothers to coach their partners before labor to avoid such a scene, the two advised, a hint that fathers' involvement was actually more show than substance.) In truth, men were included in childbirth mostly as a symbolic gesture, a sign that they were committed to being a present, responsible father after the baby was born. It was the bond of intimacy and trust established before and during labor that was the real point of men acting as "coaches"; fathers' instructions to "relax," "breathe," and "stay focused" or wiping the perspiration from mothers' foreheads carried a deeper, longer-term purpose than supposedly easing the childbirth process.[19]

In order that men were not "left out" of the pregnancy and childbirth experience, they were encouraged to be as kind and helpful as possible to the mother. There were many opportunities for men to become as Ruth Pennebaker of *Parents* put it in 1994, "the perfect pregnant father." That man did not make jokes about his mate's weight, with bonus points awarded to those who insisted the doctor's scale was ten pounds over. Not-so-funny remarks also were not called for when the expectant lady was going through one of her many wacky food phases, like wanting to eat only Ben & Jerry's Salted Caramel ice cream or Doritos Cool Ranch tortilla chips. (My wife ate only cherry and lemon ices for days at a time.) Noting how sexy all pregnant women were was another positive thing a man could do, and there was no end to the level or kinds of pampering that could potentially be involved. Giving flowers and massages on a regular basis were certainly nice, but doing something like painting that Reubensesque woman's toenails was considered extra special. (Kevin Costner's character did just that for Susan Sarandon's character in the 1988 movie *Bull Durham*.) Finally, despite popular opinion, men were advised not to bring a video camera into the delivery room, as most women knew they would likely not be looking their best while giving birth. Need it be said, hauling in a film crew, as some proud papas did much to the surprise of the movie's star, was also a bad idea that could turn one of life's most wonderful moments into something out of a Stephen King novel.[20]

LET DADS BE DADS

Alongside the pressure for men to be an integral half of the parenting team was the growing recognition that fathers should not emulate mothers. By the early 1990s, the backlash to the decades-long effort to turn fathers into quasi-mothers was increasing in intensity. Moms were good at being moms and dads were equally proficient in being dads, more experts were coming to agree, a reversal of the gender blending that had been taking place since the late 1960s. Again, complementary child-raising skills were now considered best, a tag-team approach in which each parent brought his or her strengths to create a kind of parental synergy. Jerrold Lee Shapiro, a professor, clinical psychologist, and family therapist, was a leader in this line of thought; his views were formed after he interviewed nearly one thousand dads and observed the behavior of hundreds of families. Fathers and mothers simply did things differently, he concluded, the latter not necessarily better parents because they were female. Relegating dads to a Mr. Mom–like role was a bad idea, Shapiro felt, finding that good fathers were not simply masculine versions of their partners. "Even though we often encourage men to be more like women in bringing up their children, my research has convinced me that this is a big mistake," he wrote in *Parents* in 1994, believing instead that "what fathers offer their children is something quite different from—but just as important as—what mothers offer."[21]

How exactly did American dads differ from American moms? Fathers were especially good at offering a child protection, constancy, and freedom, Shapiro found in his study, while mothers' forte was providing that same child closeness, comfort, and a sense of togetherness. These differences were expressed in various ways, via physical contact, play, discipline, and communication. Within the area of physical contact, fathers tended to put some space between themselves and their children (sometimes literally by tossing them like footballs into the air), while moms typically clung closely to them. With respect to play, dads usually served as a teacher of a particular activity, while moms typically took part at the child's level. When some sort of discipline was needed, fathers' inclination was to use a set of rules, whereas mothers were more flexible and made their decision about what to do based on the particular situation. (Neither parent was now likely to spank a child; physical punishment was seen as less a legitimate form of discipline than a form of child abuse.)[22] Finally, fathers communicated with their kids in a short and sweet manner, while mothers used emotional language (and significantly more of it) in conversations. Fathers were not simply substitute mothers, Shapiro concluded, making a public call to "let dads be dads" for the benefit of all parties.[23]

The differences between fathers and mothers reached almost back to the point of conception, experts suggested. That it was the female who carried the baby "delay[ed] a man's complete acceptance of impending fatherhood," wrote Nancy Seid and Annis Golden in *Parents*, with most fathers-to-be experiencing a considerable amount of pressure through their partner's pregnancy. The coming responsibility to protect and provide for the child kept many a dad-to-be up at night, agreed Shapiro, who had written a book titled *When Men Are Pregnant*. The idea of "pregnant dads" was substantive enough to spark a literary mini-genre; Martin Greenberg's *The Birth of a Father*, Jack Heinowitz's *Pregnant Fathers*, and Armin A. Brott and Jennifer Ash's *The Expectant Father* each explored the complex range of emotions fathers were said to experience during their partner's pregnancy.[24] Although they were not reluctant to play with their child as if he or she was part of the Flying Wallendas, dads were actually more nervous than moms when it came to trusting other caregivers with their babies. For example, fathers' concern for the welfare of their kids was greater than that of mothers when sending them to daycare or playschool, one study reported in *Psychological Science*. The dads felt more separation anxiety than moms when leaving their toddler at childcare, the group of psychologists who led the study found to their surprise, another example of fathers' undervalued emotional investment in parenthood.[25]

A WORLD WITHOUT FATHERS

Researchers' taking a closer look at fathers' role in the family was part of a bigger cultural shift regarding men. The mid-1990s represented a key juncture for male identity, in fact, with men—especially dads—urged to embrace responsibility and commitment in all its forms. Some in the media began to label 1994 "The Year of the Father" in recognition of this scrutinizing of men and because of the social and political impact of the fatherhood movement.[26] The concern over absentee fathers was especially alarming, considered an egregious abandonment of men's accountability. Based on some of the things they were each up to, both President Clinton and Vice President Gore appeared to be fully aware of the political power of the issue. Gore was the host of a July 1994 symposium that focused on the role of men in children's lives, putting him in the spotlight as one of the country's "model" fathers (a claim he summarily dismissed). For the vice president, fatherhood was in his words "the most important role that any of us will ever play in life," admonishing men who wanted little or no part of that role after having a child with a woman.[27]

One of Gore's major initiatives within the arena of fatherhood was to try to change corporate America's attitudes toward families, particularly employees' much-sought balance between work and spending time with their kids. (Gore himself had four children and claimed to have found such a balance despite his busy job.) Over time and with some serious pushing, the vice president argued, companies had evolved when it came to the issues of race and gender but lagged when it came to the interests of families. A similar movement to civil rights or women's rights was needed, he felt, with government able to push employers in the right direction. (The Family and Medical Leave Act, which entitled employees to take unpaid, job-protected leave for certain family and medical reasons, was passed in 1993.) One of Gore's pet ideas was to launch a "Father to Father" program modeled after the Mother to Mother program operated by the Disciples of Christ. "Successful" fathers would be teamed up with men who were having a tough time being good dads, his concept went, something that would benefit not just the men but their kids. Meanwhile, something called Fathernet— an "electronic forum" for fathers to communicate with each other and share ideas—could be found on the Internet (which, contrary to urban mythology, Al Gore did not invent or even claim to have invented). The vice president was also in favor of public high schools making mandatory a family-related course in order to better prepare young adults for raising children—a step clearly intended to lower the probability of fathers opting out of involvement in their kids' lives.[28]

Gore's ideas were in retrospect a bit too ambitious (the Father to Father program never really took off), but they were well justified given the prevalence of fatherlessness in the United States. Almost 40 percent of American children did not live with their fathers in 1995, a statistic too shocking to go ignored. (The number had more than doubled since 1960.) More research was showing the correlation between the presence of a biological father and his child's relative success and happiness (regardless of income or race), reason enough for the growing movement to try to keep or put dads together with their kids. Even more compelling, many of the country's social problems appeared to be linked with fatherlessness, elevating the seriousness of the issue. "Fatherlessness is the most destructive trend of our generation," said David Blankenhorn, author of the new book *Fatherless America: Confronting Our Most Urgent Social Problem*, clearly of the belief that something had to be done and done fast to avoid a national calamity. A missing father was a better predictor of criminal activity than race or poverty, Blankenhorn showed, a surprising fact likely to make anyone involved in the legal system rethink how best to discourage crime. A couple staying together was a better deterrent to breaking the law than hiring additional police, rather incredibly, meaning there was a financial incentive as well to keep fathers in the picture. Both positive activities (i.e., education, employment) and negative ones (teenage pregnancy, drug usage, suicide) were connected with fatherhood, according to the data, countering critics spouting off about the superfluousness of a male parent beyond his reproductive ability.[29]

Blankenhorn went further in his treatise on the importance of fathers. While mothers tended to focus on a child's current needs, whether physical or emotional, fathers contributed to his or her development in a broader, longer-term sense. Kids were likely to gain such attributes as independence, self-reliance, and a tolerance for risk taking from dads, he argued, implying that a fatherless family put limitations on child development. And like others who made the case that all dads were not created equal, Blankenhorn found fault with those fathers who were not fully committed to the job. The "Unnecessary Father" could be useful but had little real impact, he felt, while the "Visiting Father" was good only from a financial sense. Then there was the "Sperm Father," whose contribution to parenting was purely biological, and the collectively grouped "Stepfather and the Nearby Guy," each a man who often did more harm than good. It was only the "Good Family Man" who delivered the full paternal goods, Blankenhorn explained, that man making the welfare of his wife and kids his biggest priority in life.[30] And just to be clear, child-support payments were no replacement for fatherhood, he added, the media's recent attention to deadbeat dads largely missing the point. Of course fathers should contribute monetarily to raising a child, Blankenhorn wrote in *National Review* in 1995, but their presence in the home was the far more important issue.[31]

Others agreed that despite the rise of the "new fatherhood," the state of the American dad had not improved in recent decades given the startling rise of fatherlessness. In his 1996 *Life Without Father*, David Popenoe, a professor of sociology at Rutgers, considered the rise of fatherlessness as "one of the most unexpected and extraordinary social trends," and a major cause of "some of the most disturbing problems that plague society." One could argue about the implications, but there was no debate that fatherlessness had become much more common in the United States. From 1960 to 1990, the percentage of children not living with their biological fathers had risen from 17 to 36 percent, Popenoe pointed out, echoing others' analysis of the data. The worse news was that the numbers were not getting any better, making him and other social critics very worried about the nation's future. As Blankenhorn posited, fatherlessness was linked to crime, teen pregnancy, substance abuse, poverty, and other problems, with nothing less than a "calamity" waiting in the wings. The au courant view that fathers were largely "unnecessary" was not all true, Popenoe argued, seeing the presence of dads in the home as essential to a healthy society. "If we are to make progress toward a more just and humane society, we must reverse the tide that is pulling fathers apart from their families," he concluded, seeing nothing as "more important for our children or for our future as a nation."[32]

While some maintained that fatherhood was experiencing a historic high as men strove for parental equality, equally loud voices argued that it was falling to a new low in terms of actual numbers. Various groups subscribing to the latter point of view were firmly committed to erasing the country's dubious distinction of having the world's highest rate of father absence. Importantly, the drive to do something about absent fathers crossed political and social lines, with both conservatives and liberals as well as the religious and secular dedicated to the cause. In addition to the National Fatherhood Initiative (NFI), the Kansas-based National Center for Fathering was taking a leadership role in the field, specifically by teaching men how to be good fathers. The nonprofit was led by Ken Canfield, who was using his own book, *The Seven Secrets of Effective Fathers*, as the model by which to train aspiring dads. Minority outreach was a particular focus of Canfield's, with prisoners, military personnel, and inner-city men targeted to attend the organization's two-day seminars.[33]

Although not a true fatherhood group, the Christian evangelical organization Promise Keepers was also doing what it could to strengthen marriages and families. Tens of thousands of men were filling sports arenas (at fifty-five dollars a head) to be part of a revival-like experience for two days, much of the inspirational goings-on centered around the joys and responsibilities of fatherhood. Others groups included the Fatherhood Project ("a national research and education program to increase male involvement in childrearing"), the Institute for Responsible Fatherhood and Family Revitalization (a bible-based effort to reunite African American men with their children), the Fathers' Education Network (a Detroit-based program for ex-cons), and M.A.D.–D.A.D.S. (Men Against Destruction—Defending Against Drugs and Social Disorder). That group's ambitious goal was to turn drug dealers and gang members into responsible men and fathers, often confronting the bad guys right on the street in the wee hours of the morning. In addition to those resources, there was no shortage of new books devoted to male parenting, including Henry B. Biller and Robert J. Trotter's *The Father Factor: What You Need to Know to Make a Difference*, Doug Spangler's *Fatherhood: An Owner's Manual*, Aaron Hass's *The Gift of Fatherhood*, and Paul Lewis's *The Five Key Habits of Smart Dads*.[34]

If Blankenhorn and Popenoe served as the most passionate messengers warning of the dangers of absentee fatherhood, Wade Horn of the NFI was the man who was most eager to do something about it. As president of that organization, Horn was a one-man army fighting for the cause of fatherhood, locating it within the constellation of traditional values. What he termed "the fatherhood ideal" had been all but dead, Horn believed, but it was now making a major comeback as people realized the importance of the two-parent (male-female) family. Divorce and illegitimacy had since the 1960s taken a serious toll on the well-being of children, he held, a disturbing trend obscured by the (liberal) push for social androgyny. In such a cultural climate, it was not surprising that fathers became seen as nonessential, a conclusion supported by what Horn called "radical feminist rhetoric." ("A woman needs a man like a fish needs a bicycle," Gloria Steinem had famously said.) If that were not enough, there was a growing belief that children were quite resilient and could typically withstand changes in family structure without any real psychological or emotional trauma.[35]

In the early nineties, however, the tide began to turn against all of these negative influences, Horn was happy to report, with some sanity restored to the national conversation about the role of fathers. (Horn actually traced the spark of the fatherhood movement to Dan Quayle's 1992 infamous "Murphy Brown" speech, when the vice president criticized the sassy television character's choice to be a single mom. It was, more likely, an offshoot of the concurrent "men's movement" led by Robert Bly.) The fatherhood movement galvanized over the next few years, spurred on by a slew of articles and books that supported the ideas that fathers were a critical component of not just a happy home but a healthy society. Initiatives, programs, and activism—much of it sponsored by the NFI—followed, resulting in some success in fathers making a renewed commitment to family life. As well, more robust efforts were being made to chase down deadbeat dads, providing usually much-needed financial assistance for single moms. On the brink of extinction, in Horn's view, "the fatherhood ideal" had been saved just in time.[36]

THE BASEBALL DAD

Although obviously informed by a conservative strain of politics, the fatherhood movement was grounded in a larger conversation about gender roles in America. The "soccer mom" had recently and quickly entered the cultural lexicon, so much so that it became the (not very flattering) label of a particular target audience that each candidate strove to appeal to in the 1996 presidential campaign. The male equivalent was the "baseball dad," a man that Ann Hulbert of the *New Republic* described as a father who "schedules his paid job . . . around the time-consuming avocation of coaching a little league team of fourth graders." (Fathers were actually quite involved in soccer coaching, even more so than moms.) While the "baseball dad" conjured up the image of a minivan-driving father overly concerned with whether his son (or daughter) could hit a curveball, it certainly was a more favorable archetype than the "angry white male" of the early 1990s. Baseball dads were also seen as less "pushy" than soccer moms, with some gender bias no doubt in play. The former viewed his coaching job as a fun escape from the pressures of work, it was popularly believed, while the latter was an insufferable presence on the sidelines, haranguing all parties on the field (especially the refs) before moving on to the next activity on her child's busy schedule. Both Democrat Bill Clinton and Republican Bob Dole visibly wore baseball caps during their campaign, in fact, a move seen by some pundits as a symbolic attempt to woo both baseball dads and their soccer mom wives. Clinton looked far more natural as a baseball dad, everyone agreed, with Dole coming off more like a surly umpire.[37]

New research confirmed that dads, whether coaching baseball or otherwise, were, again, quite different from moms and added a vital component to the child-raising process. Fathers contributed humor and excitement with their physical form of play, something that was believed to lead to a greater sense of self-control and social relationships later in life for a child. Moms protected their kids from exhilaration while dads encouraged it, this polarity pushing children to expand their emotional range. Fathers were far more likely "to get children worked up, negatively or positively, with fear as well as delight," explained Michael Lamb, a psychologist and research director at the National Institute for Child Health and Human Development, this energetic and vigorous form of interaction "forcing them to learn to regulate their feelings." As well, children developed a more complex set of communication and problem-solving skills from their dads, the latest studies showed, assets that paid off big dividends down the road.[38]

On a grander level, fathers' greater involvement with their kids illustrated some of the sweeping changes in American society over the past generation or two. For Jerry Adler of *Newsweek*, upon comparing his role as parent with that of his own dad, fatherhood had gotten twice as complex (and twice as hard) since the 1950s. Each had to make a living, but his father never went hiking with his kids, sewed them costumes for a school pageant, or made marinara sauce with them from scratch, all things Adler had done. While fathers were effectively assigned this dual role, it was important to keep in mind that men of previous generations never were really permitted to share such activities with their kids. The doubling down of the American dad was thus a blessing of sorts, an opportunity to establish relationships with their children that could help men themselves grow as human beings. Baby boomers were embracing this opportunity with full gusto, seeing child raising as an ideal vehicle of personal transformation. "Baby boomers have transformed paternity, as they have every other institution they have touched, into an all-consuming vocation and never-ending quest for improvement and self-fulfillment," Adler wrote, with many men viewing fatherhood as one more aspect of life to master.[39]

Baby boomers' other reason to approach fatherhood like it was a triathlon was to make up for the lack of attachment with their own dads. Men of the 1950s were not known for their emotionality, including that expressed between their children, and fathers of the 1990s appeared to be determined to compensate, if not overcompensate, in this regard. Quite a few dads were saying, "I love you," to their child a dozen times a day, an attempt (conscious or otherwise) to fix something in their own lives. "There is disappointment, a sense of loss, regret bordering on anger," said Don Eberley of the NFI, thinking that the recent men's movement was about addressing the alienation postwar fathers felt toward their families. Contemporary dads were known to replay words spoken (or not spoken) by their fathers over and over, wondering how their old man could have been so indifferent or insensitive. Some dads of the 1950s were not even present when their son or daughter was born, a fitting metaphor for the distance they created with their kids. Now, fathering how-tos like Canfield's, Lewis's, and John Boswell and Ron Barrett's *How to Dad* were selling briskly, books that most postwar dads likely could have used even more.[40]

Some fathers, regardless of their political affiliation, had difficulty facing the fact that the traditional gender roles of the family had imploded over the past couple of decades. More women were now the principal breadwinner (48 percent of married women brought in half or more of their family's income in 1996, according to the Families and Work Institute), leaving men with not just primary childcare responsibilities but taking the lead in house chores as well. Men who had always assumed they would contribute at least a portion of household income were feeling frustrated and bitter when it turned out it was their wives who were contributing most or all of it. While some men thus dreamed of being able to quit their stressful jobs and become stay-at-home dads, others felt a serious blow to their self-image when they were effectively forced into that position. Men and women were going in opposite directions in the workplace, a historical shift leaving in its wake a significant amount of marital stress. Interestingly, children did not care which parent made more money; their priority was getting emotional support from both mom and dad rather than which one brought home the proverbial bacon.[41]

As gender roles in the family further scrambled, new studies added to the growing body of research that fathers and mothers approached parenting quite differently. Whereas moms leaned heavily toward being a caregiver and "general manager," the dads preferred to be their child's, for lack of a better word, playmate. As well, mothers emphasized verbal and intellectual interaction (talking, singing, or reading) while fathers were much more likely to engage in rough-and-tumble physical activity with their son or daughter. The distinction carried over to the playground; moms often sat on benches with other moms watching their kids play while dads typically jumped into the fray. Sheldon Himelfarb, a National Public Radio commentator, was taken aback by the amount of stuff (juice, milk, snacks, extra diapers, a change of clothes, and Band-Aids) women took to his local playground in Washington, as he simply brought a ball for his daughter to play with. And while the moms "shared intelligence on everything from schools to stretch marks," he and the rest of the dads engaged in a rather aggressive and competitive kind of play.[42] Men were also more apt to do personal things—watch television, eat, or work out (sometimes all at the same time)—while taking care of a kid (or two), this multitasking not always appreciated by women. Moms also found dads' penchant to dress their children in clothes that looked just like daddy's rather odd and somewhat disturbing.[43] Experts continued to view these different approaches as beneficial to child development, however, and perhaps served as a reminder that the more things changed in terms of gender blending, the more they remained the same.[44]

THE FATHERHOOD INDUSTRY

If Al Gore was considered the archetypical model father in the mid-1990s, his boss filled that role at the end of the decade. Despite the revelation that he likely had had many extramarital affairs, no one arguably better illustrated the power of the fatherhood image in the public's imagination than Bill Clinton. Part of that simply had to do with policy making. The president had in 1995 asked all the executive departments and agencies within his administration to include fathers in their programs and policies, something obviously long overdue. To the federal government, fathers had long been the "hidden parent," his role in family life perceived as limited to that of breadwinner. With Clinton's directive, however, the government increasingly acknowledged that fathers played an instrumental role in children's development; the move not only had major, long-term consequences but made the president, in the public's eye, a champion of the American dad.[45]

There was more to it, however. In the spring of 1998, President Clinton was hardly out of the woods from "Monicagate" yet his approval ratings were up, cause to speculate on why. The economy was chugging along nicely—almost always a boost for a president's likability—but some political observers suspected there was another, more psychological reason. Writing in the *New Republic*, Peter Rubin presented the idea that Clinton had (intentionally or otherwise) assumed the role of "national dad," a persona that was working in his favor. Save for his more vocal critics, the president was popularly seen as "a member of the family," Rubin argued, this serving as a kind of buffer during the scandal. That Clinton was a strong advocate for initiatives related to families only furthered his image as the ultimate American dad and helped to shield him from negative criticism. One had to go back to Ronald Reagan in the mid-1980s—specifically, his moving televised address after the Challenger disaster—to recall such a recognizable "national dad," Rubin believed, proof perhaps that the positive aspects of fatherhood transcended ideology or politics.[46]

Bill Clinton may have been the most well-known American dad, but many moms genuinely believed their husband was the best. When *Parents* magazine asked readers to submit essays explaining why the father of the family was outstanding, 5,200 entries poured in, a number surprising even to the editors. Judging by the response, the country was virtually overflowing with what the magazine called "dream dads," making the selection of the best five a difficult one. "Who knew the world was so full of superheroes?" the editors asked, a good question given the kind of stories women shared. There seemed to be no limit to the outpourings of love and acts of sacrifice fathers had made for the sake of their children, each of the five winners a source of inspiration for others. One dad from Wake Forest, North Carolina, resigned from his teaching job in order to take care of his eighteen-month-old son; another from Chicago dedicated "his heart, his soul, and his being" to his daughter; a third from Rockport, Massachusetts, spent every moment he could with his little girl, who had a genetic disease; another from Oak Park, Michigan, was "best buddies" with his son; and the last from Scottsdale, Arizona, loved his adopted two-year-old twin girls from the very second he laid eyes on them. While no doubt a fluff piece (the magazine was, after all, the loudest cheerleader for good parenting), the article also served as a resounding retort to the unrelenting reports in the media about absentee or deadbeat dads, and as a reminder that there was no shortage of great fathers around.[47]

With fatherhood experiencing a cultural zenith of sorts, celebrities seized the opportunity to tell their personal stories of being a dad. Paul Reiser, the costar of the popular television show *Mad About You*, was obviously channeling Bill Cosby and his 1986 bestseller *Fatherhood* with his own book, *Babyhood*. (Reiser had had a hit a few years earlier with his previous book, *Couplehood*.) In *Babyhood*, another *New York*

Times bestseller, the actor told the usual fish-out-of-water stories of having a first child—bringing the baby home from the hospital, their dog's reaction upon learning there was literally a new kid in town, the different parenting styles between him and his wife, and how his life had changed since having his son Ezra. Nothing in the book was extraordinary or even particularly interesting, but there seemed to be no limit to readers' interest in how famous people were handling fatherhood, perhaps because they were having the same kind of experiences everyone else was. [48]

Because of their fame and success, celebrities also served as handy role models for a positive interpretation of fatherhood. Whether their stories were true or not (many magazine articles were no doubt orchestrated by publicists), a fair number of famous men were presented as great fathers despite their busy schedules and tendency to be away from home for considerable amounts of time. The bond between actor Jimmy Smits and his fifteen-year-old son Kino "transcends distance," as *People* magazine described it in 1998, putting a positive spin on what was not an ideal situation. Not only was Smits no longer together with the mother of Kino, but he lived in Los Angeles while she and his son lived in New York. Still, Smits was able to spend "school breaks and occasional weekends" with Kino, this along with their genetic connection accounting for their claimed closeness. Tony Danza and his wife had also split up, but he remained close with his son Marc, *People* told readers, another example of a father overcoming the challenges of a Hollywood career and lifestyle to successfully play, as Al Gore had put it, "the most important role that any of us will ever play in life." [49]

If the celebrity-oriented media was a fair judge, the variety of famous, wonderful fathers was truly amazing, as was their joy in becoming dads. "Hollywood's freshly minted papas can't stop singing the praises of baby love," gushed *People* in 1999, with "masculine pride bursting out all over" Tinsel Town. It was as if no man had ever before become a father. "We call him the scoodle bug," said Christian Slater of his new son, Jaden, describing him as "a miracle in my life." (The actor had recently served time in jail on drug and battery charges.) Richie Sambora, the guitarist of the rock band Bon Jovi, admitted he was "well-versed in Barney" after having a baby with his equally famous wife, Heather Locklear. Besides being able to sing the purple dinosaur's (truly cloying) theme song ("I Love You"), Sambora claimed he could fasten a Pampers in twenty seconds. *People* wittily described Sambora and Slater as prime examples of a "grateful dad," that is, men who had a totally other side to their tough-guy image and were fully appreciative of it.[50]

Judging by the outpouring of celebrities' stories about their dads, fatherhood was indeed "hot right now," as Judith Davidoff of the *Progressive* put it.[51] Retired boxer Jake LaMotta told his story in *Esquire*, explaining how his father played an instrumental role in choosing his profession. When LaMotta returned to his home in the Bronx beaten up by an older kid one day, his father told him to "never run away from nobody" and emphasized the point by handing him an ice pick should he run into trouble again. The weapon came in handy a few days later, when he slashed the face of a boy who attacked him. "I guess you could say my father and growin' up in the Bronx made me a fighter," LaMotta understatedly remarked. The comedian Jerry Stiller also had a rough childhood and paid similar credit to his father for turning him into the success he was. "Everything I did came from him," he said, something Stiller found ironic given that his dad "never laughed at anything I did." (At age 101, a year before he died, Stiller's father did tell his son that he "turned out good.") Stiller admitted he had not been the best dad, missing both his daughter Amy's and son Ben's births because of work, but took pride that he must have done something right given how each turned out.[52]

THE DADDY TRAP

Stiller's struggle to find a proper balance between work and family would, by the end of the century, become an all-too-common complaint. More fathers were experiencing "daddy stress," as it was sometimes known, perhaps because of the greater expectations to embrace both the joys and responsibilities of "the new fatherhood." The terms of fatherhood had changed drastically in the last half century, but many men had jobs not unlike those in the 1950s, with little opportunity to disappear from the office during a weekday (or even an evening or weekend) to spend time with a child. The pressure to be both a great employee and a great dad was bubbling over into not just stress but guilt, depression, bad work performance, and divorce, not unlike what many mothers experienced a generation earlier when they embarked on full-time careers. In fact, a contributing factor to "daddy stress" was that both parents in a household held full-time jobs, making it difficult for either one to invest a lot of time in childcare during the week. Many employers were somewhat lenient about female employees having to look after kids on company time but significantly less so about men, a legacy of traditional gender roles. More enlightened companies were offering new fathers paternity leave, but many men refused to take it, thinking that if they did they would pay a heavy price in terms of their career path.[53]

Observing the same trend in the late nineties, *Business Week* described the work versus family dilemma as the "Daddy Trap," something in which more men appeared to be getting caught. Some fathers were hardly seeing their children during the week because of early mornings and late evenings at work and, sadly, sensed they would later in life regret it. These men felt not just stress but conflict and guilt about how they prioritized their time, emotions they were reluctant to reveal to their employers or wives for fear it could be damaging at work or home. "Balance" had become a buzzword in the self-help arena, an outgrowth of Eastern and New Age philosophy, but many dads were fully aware they had precious little of it in their lives. Fathers of a previous generation looked at the phenomenon with amazement at how anyone could pull off such a tricky balancing act and considered themselves lucky they had not been placed between such a rock and hard place because of the prevailing gender roles. Men justified their long hours at work as for the greater good of the family because of the money being brought into the household, but this did not ease their troubled consciences. Turning down promotions was one way men tried to strike a balance between work and family ("I'm going to be a father longer than I'll be a working man," said one), but this was hardly an optimal solution to the problem.[54]

Widespread "daddy stress" and falling into a "daddy trap" did little, however, to diminish the expectation for men to play an active part in their children's lives. As the century drew to a close, the fatherhood movement appeared to be reaching a kind of critical mass as Americans sought to quell their millennium jitters with sources of stability. The NFI, which had been formed in 1994, was on a roll, gaining followers with its message that "fathers make unique and irreplaceable contribu-

tions to the lives of their children." The organization was running a
commercial on network television produced by the Ad Council that was
designed to prevent fathers from becoming, as they were often called,
"wayward dads."[55] The ad suggested that fatherhood was a fundamental
aspect of animal behavior, human or otherwise:

> (Over the visual of a herd of elephants) When young bull elephants
> from a national park in South Africa were moved to different loca-
> tions without the presence of an adult male, they began to wantonly
> kill other animals. When an adult male was relocated with them, the
> delinquent behavior stopped.

> (Over the visual of an African American hugging a child on a basket-
> ball court) Without the influence of their dads, kids are more likely
> to get into trouble, too. Just a reminder how important it is for
> fathers to spend time with their children.[56]

Backed by the call for welfare reform in Washington, the NFI was in
an ideal position to both get its message across and gain political clout.
The organization was pushing hard for state laws that would favor married couples in education and housing, an unapologetic (and seemingly
unconstitutional) swipe at single parents. While the NFI was clearly an
extreme example, mainstream organizations such as the Ford Foundation as well as the federal government were promoting various "responsible fatherhood" programs. Single moms had been the focus of welfare
reform in the early 1990s, but now it was dads who were, according to
conservatives and even some liberals, not fulfilling their familial obligations. Senators Evan Bayh (D-Indiana) and Pete Domenici (R-New
Mexico) had recently sponsored a bill called the Responsible Fatherhood Act that, if passed, would award more than $150 million in federal
funds to pro-fatherhood projects. While the bill died in Congress, it
illustrated the full-scale attack on absentee fathers that was taking
place.[57]

While the concern over "wayward" dads was almost universal, a rare
contrarian voice to the perils of the absentee father appeared in a June
1999 article in *American Psychologist*. In their "Reconstructing the Essential Father," Louise Silverstein and Carl Auerbach made the rather
stunning argument that "neither a mother nor a father is essential" for
raising a well-adjusted child, a direct challenge to popular belief. A two-

parent, heterosexual marriage was not the only basis for a happy, healthy family, they held after a thorough analysis of the empirical literature, making the case that the structure of a household was less important than the warmth and consistency found within it. Conservatives (including Rush Limbaugh) immediately condemned the coauthors of the study (each a professor at Yeshiva University), seeing their work as an assault on fatherhood itself. Another study showed, however, that it was better for a child to be with a single mom if the two shared a good relationship than to be in a two-parent household where the child's relationship with his or her dad was not particularly good. Was the fatherhood movement built on false assumptions about the importance of fathers in a family? Was it enough for a child to have a loving relationship with his or her mother alone?[58]

Such questions needed to be asked because of the Mixmastering of the American family over the course of the twentieth century. Regardless of conservatives' unwavering faith in traditional marriage, single fathers, surrogate fathers, stepfathers, "social" dads, long-distance dads, and serial dads were all now part of the familial equation. Frederic Golden and Annie Murphy Paul of *Psychology Today* called the current version of family life "postmodern parenting," a nice way to describe the scrambling of roles and relationships.[59] Another key question revolved around whether fathers had indeed gone through a major transformation (for the better), as many social critics claimed. Margaret Carlson, a columnist for *Time*, was skeptical, believing men were, as the saying went, men. Carlson had serious doubts about the validity of a survey by the Families and Work Institute that reported fathers were spending significantly more time with their families than twenty years ago. "Have husbands really evolved from hunters and gatherers into nurturers and helpmates?" she asked, answering, "I don't think so." It remained women who kept the household going, she was firmly convinced, with men getting undue credit for their domestic contributions. Whether it was doing chores, taking part in school activities, or deciding which parent stayed home with a sick child, it was the mom rather than the dad who still bore the heavy responsibility. "Men are pulling a fast one on these gullible pollsters," Carlson concluded, of the opinion that "the new fatherhood" was significantly more sizzle than steak.[60] Such questions about men's role as fathers were not about to go away, as the

American dad embarked on yet another new course along his fascinating journey.

4

THE ROLE OF A LIFETIME

The truth is, the simple act of becoming a dad, whether stay-at-home
or otherwise, is transformative.
                              —Michael Snider, a new dad, 2005

Father's Day was fast approaching, and Michael Snider had good reason to rejoice. This would be the first Father's Day that Snider, a researcher and writer, would celebrate as a dad, an event in which he
unabashedly reveled. Snider now had an eleven-month-old daughter,
Chloe, and felt the need to share his feelings with readers. Snider's
wife, Tammy, had had a difficult pregnancy and even tougher labor, he
explained, making the occasion that much more blissful. Chloe's birth
was "the most glorious moment of my life," Snider exclaimed, a sentiment father after father has expressed throughout time. Now having
"the most beautiful baby you've ever seen," the man was clearly smitten
with the girl, taking a few months off from his job to take care of her
while his wife went back to work. He had also changed his behavior in
some respects, driving more slowly and giving teenage boys the evil eye
even though Chloe was a decade and a half away from her first potential
date. "It's hard to admit in today's society, where status and career
occupy such importance, but being a father defines me," Snider wrote,
claiming that for him "every day is father's day."[1]

Snider's feelings about fatherhood, while particularly effusive, were
not unlike those of many dads in the first decade of the twenty-first
century. For the last twenty years or so, men had come to embrace their
role as fathers, seeing it as the cornerstone of who they were as people.

As well, men were increasingly rejecting the model of fatherhood predicated on motherhood, carving out a paternal identity that affirmed, rather than denied, their masculinity. Guided by a variety of social forces, including the aging of the baby boomers, fatherhood was apt to be described as "the role of a lifetime," the most important and fulfilling experience a man could have. Fathers were more involved with their children than ever before, continuing their ascent as parents. As they devoted more time and energy to parenting, dads received more attention in the media, a sign that they were considered instrumental to child raising. Still, many fathers believed they were largely neglected or disregarded, not getting nearly the respect of mothers despite their obvious commitment to their kids (deadbeat dads aside). It was clear that the American dad had made great progress but had some way to go before he was awarded the same social status as the American mom.

DADDY'S BIG MOMENT

As the nation entered a new century, it was clear that the popularity of and attention to fathers in the 1990s was not just a passing fad. In fact, it was, according to Amy Dickinson of *Time*, "daddy's big moment," with new magazines, websites, and books targeted to fathers who wanted to be better parents to their child or children. A magazine called *Dads* had just appeared on newsstands ("the lifestyle magazine for today's fathers"), as did *Dad's Magazine*, this too targeted to men seeking more meaningful relationships with their children. (Simply being recognized as a legitimate market can be seen as a form of respect.) Unlike dads of previous generations, however, twenty-first-century fathers had no intention of being a male version of mothers. "Instead of becoming a 'mom in drag,' the new dad wants to integrate his 'guyness' into his life as a father," Dickinson noted, resulting in a bending and stretching of the techniques and concept of parenthood. Fathers were, in some cases, encroaching on the territory of mothers, in the process breaking some of the accepted rules for how to raise a child. More progressive women celebrated men's intensified interest in parenting, allowing and even encouraging them to do things their own way. Children would be the primary beneficiaries of two gender-specific caregivers, they understood, with studies showing that kids thrived under a complementary parental system.[2]

Despite the research indicating that fathers contributed mightily to their children's development, however, the American dad was still often viewed as a second-class parent and a victim of gender bias. "Harassed and belittled by the left, straightjacketed and ignored by the right, the dutiful American dad can't win no matter how much he tries to please his critics," wrote Cathy Young in the *American Spectator* in 2000. There had of course been many changes in parenthood over the past couple of decades, much of that due to men, yet childcare remained primarily a maternal domain. In divorce cases, for example, mothers were still favored heavily; they were still much more likely than fathers to receive the custodial arrangements they each believed were fair. (Mothers now retained custody 85 percent of the time.) As well, absentee and deadbeat dads made headlines, but the truth was that the vast majority of employed divorced men paid all or most of the child support they owed. (Turning the "deadbeat dad" on its head, divorced men who believed they were disenfranchised from their children because of the legal system sometimes referred to themselves as "beat-dead dads.") Feminists especially tended to be critical of the state of fatherhood in the United States, inclined to focus on the problems while ignoring the considerable advancements men had made in parenting. "There are plenty of men who are doing a wonderful job, either as traditional breadwinner fathers, or as 'nurturing dads' who are equal or even primary caregivers," Young declared, thinking that was not the general perception in the country.[3]

Feeling ignored or the object of favoritism, an increasing number of fathers were joining support groups to be part of a community and share their frustrations. Men complained that they were seen as unimportant parents and were treated by the legal system as enemies. The archetype of the dad as bumbling fool on television sitcoms had only intensified the problem, making some think that there was at least a bit of Homer Simpson in every man. Social services were certainly stacked heavily toward the interests of women, a reflection of the widespread belief that men were psychologically resilient and could deal with emotionally challenging situations by themselves. This was all the more unjust given the persistent stream of research demonstrating the value of fathers in child development. The presence of dads in family life helped boys develop relationships outside the trajectory of their mothers, it had recently been shown, as well as discouraged girls from engaging in premature sexual activity. Fathers instilled healthy competition among both boys and girls, studies also revealed, something that made kids more likely to want to achieve things in life. Fatherhood had been transformed dramatically over the past couple of decades, but American society had not kept up with these changes, it was fair to say, a product of enduring gender stereotypes.[4]

Benedict Carey, who placed himself somewhere between a part-time and full-time dad, definitely felt like he was the source of some belittling. Neighbors looked at him suspiciously while he spent days at home with his two-year-old daughter, wondering why he was not at work like his wife. Until recently a successful journalist, Carey decided to be the primary caregiver when his wife landed a much better paying job. Carey envisioned himself being able to continue his writing career while he watched his little girl, something that turned out not to be true. "The only project I've been working on is how to get through a day," he explained, and that was with the help of a full-time babysitter. Carey's situation was much like those of other men who believed they would be able to keep their careers going while chasing their kids around the house. "It didn't last long," said a lawyer from Illinois with two sons, speaking of his legal practice. After trying to work from home, the man conceded that, "the boys are now my career," a conclusion he had reached gradually as it became clear that he could not do each job well. Men in this position were happy with their decision but were not sure what to say when asked what they did for a living, wondering if they should refer to their career in the present or past tense. Not quite comfortable with each of these options, full-time dads would get to the point where they could say they stayed home to take care of their kids, a source of much relief after struggling with self-definition.[5]

Part-time dads were in some sense in a tougher spot than such full-timers. Fathers whose partners worked longer hours and made more money typically did morning and early evening shifts with the kids, with their own, less-demanding (and lower-paying) jobs sandwiched in between. For them, not just time was an issue, but money. Taught to be breadwinners, these men found themselves having to ask their wives for an allowance, quite a blow to their pride. "My wife is a doctor, and occasionally I feel like a loser, a sponge, like I've thrown in the towel," said a computer programmer from California who took the parental lead in the family. While the daily grind was formidable, it was the loss of identity that really threw part-time dads for a loop; some were not quite sure who they were anymore. Creating a new self that had a decidedly lower professional component took some doing, particularly for men who dreamt of going to the top of their chosen field. And once one dropped out of the fast track, it was mighty difficult getting back onto it. Gaps in resumes were a big problem for those men who wanted to reenter the workforce after leaving jobs to be primary caregivers to children; this was the very same challenge millions of women had faced. Men and women still face challenges reentering the workplace after choosing to be full-time parents, it should be noted, meaning more family-friendly employment policies could benefit both fathers and mothers.[6]

While part-time fathers considered themselves neither here or there, stay-at-home dads remained the most extreme examples of the new kind of fatherhood that emerged about twenty years earlier. There were 105,000 such fathers in the United States taking care of some 189,000 children under age fifteen, according to the first Census counting of them in 2002. While that number was not huge (experts believed there were many more than officially reported), more stay-at-home dads (or SAHDs) were popping up as unemployment rose in the early 2000s recession and as women's salaries gradually caught up to those of men. For some, the SAHD phenomenon was nothing less than revolutionary. Stay-at-home dads were "pioneers" who were rewriting the rules of manhood by prioritizing "relationships over productivity and competition," thought Terrence Real, a family therapist and author.[7] Hollywood, however, often depicted the stay-at-home dad quite differently, clinging to the silly "Mr. Mom" archetype in films such as *Big Daddy* of 1999 (starring Adam Sandler) and *Daddy Day Care* of 2003 (starring Eddie Murphy). The 2001 movie *Life as a House* (starring Kevin Kline), meanwhile, focused on the tried-and-true theme of men suddenly realizing the joys of fatherhood after experiencing some sort of life-altering event.[8]

Television, in fact, now appeared to be more in touch with reality when it came to fatherhood. On *NYPD Blue*, for example, lead character (and widower) Andy Sipowicz routinely had to find a babysitter when he had to work overtime, and the final scenes of shows often involved him reading a bedtime story to his son Theo. A new show, *The Education of Max Bickford*, starred Richard Dreyfuss as another widower, a throwback to the days of motherless television shows like *My Three Sons*, *Bonanza*, *The Andy Griffith Show*, and *The Courtship of Eddie's Father*. In the (short-lived) show, Dreyfuss played a history professor at a women's college where his daughter was a student (he also had a younger son), providing ample opportunity for interesting parental situations. In another new show, *The Guardian*, a corporate attorney finds himself a legal advocate for children after being arrested for drug possession. While not a father himself, the lawyer takes on the responsibility of caring for children through his hours of community service, another Hollywood-type story of paternal resurrection.[9]

While ex-druggies becoming dedicated surrogate dads was certainly a stretch, real-life fathers were to some extent trying to confront paternal issues of their past. Significant numbers of both baby boomers and Generation Xers wanted little to do with the good-provider-but-often-absent model of fatherhood. Many men said in plain terms that they wanted to be a better father than the one they had, and that they had every intention of being closer to their children.[10] Having another income in the family enabled men to spend more time with their children, shifting the bedrock of parenting. Also in major flux was the definition of masculinity; no longer was testosterone viewed as the chief determinant of maleness. (Good dads, in fact, had low levels of testosterone, new studies were showing, meaning there appeared to be a biological component to fatherhood just as there was for motherhood. Women experienced hormonal changes during pregnancy that triggered feelings of love for their child and the desire to nurture him or her.) Fatherhood was literally natural for men, research indicated, and masculinity much more than biologically rooted aggressive behavior.[11] As well, 10 percent of men (versus 14 percent of women) suffered from postpartum depression, a 2006 study showed, although for dads the cause was lifestyle rather than hormonal changes.[12]

Likewise, there was more anecdotal evidence suggesting that there was some kind of biological clock for men to become fathers. Childless thirtysomething men invited to hold colleagues' babies at office parties found the experience not entirely unpleasant, providing the rather startling revelation that becoming a dad could be a good thing. For both men and women of this cohort, the urge to have a baby was very much in the air in the early 2000s. Part of that had to do with Sylvia Ann Hewlett, who was making waves with her new book *Creating a Life: Professional Women and the Quest for Children*, in which she argued that many women were waiting too long to get pregnant. The biological clock was very real, more Gen X women were concluding after reading or just hearing about the book. Life priorities suddenly changed from dating to marriage and parenthood (often precisely when turning age thirty-five), a lifestyle shift to which many men appeared to relate. Seeing a child on a father's shoulders or a cutie-pie being pushed in a stroller unexpectedly triggered a heartfelt pang among a fair share of diehard bachelors, a tick of the male biological clock. Some tried to pretend they did not hear the sound, reciting all the good reasons to avoid fatherhood, but, more often than not, the bell had already tolled. [13]

THE KIND OF THING YOU LEARN ABOUT YOURSELF

For those men who decided to make the big leap, becoming a father was indeed the life-changing experience everyone told them it would be. Reading books, having nephews, or any amount of advice from veteran dads just could not prepare fathers-to-be for what was about to take place. Except in adoption situations, moms got to "know" their baby as it grew inside them for months, while this was obviously not the case for dads. It was the "foreverness" aspect of having a child that was the most frightening thing for new fathers, having little or no experience with anything that would endure for, as many had warned, "the rest of your life." [14]

Being demoted in the household was an early indication that things had been irrevocably altered after having a baby, as he or she naturally assumed the top position in terms of attention and care. (Dads as well as moms might freely admit that their love for the baby now exceeded that for each other.) Lack of sleep and the demands of an infant often strained a partnership, making romance a happy memory. Hanging out with the boys was also likely to be something enjoyed in the past, and friends without children had difficulty relating to reports of the particular digestive activity of a newborn. Pleasures once never given a second thought—watching an entire football game or reading a newspaper—

were now luxuries to be relished because they were so rare. "Nights off" were treated as mini-vacations. Longer recreational activities, such as eighteen holes of golf or a day on the boat, were not even to be considered. Along with this shrinking of fun, all kinds of safety hazards suddenly appeared out of nowhere, making dads hyper-vigilant about protecting the wee one. Who knew there were so many sharp corners in a house? they wondered, with many other dangers lurking both inside and outside presenting considerable risk to the baby's well-being.[15]

Along with all the downsides that materialized with the arrival of a baby, however, there were some definite upsides for new fathers. One's entire outlook on life was typically reoriented and for the better, many men reported, with what had been major concerns placed in proper perspective. While money was obviously important, that "big meeting" or "big report" at work no longer seemed that much of a crisis, overshadowed by the normal daily frenzy that defines taking care of an infant. The littlest of things—taking a son or daughter for a stroll or for a ride in the car—could very well zoom ahead of all the other priorities in one's personal or professional life. Many dads now wanted to be home with their child rather than at work or spending time with buddies, which was often a turning point for men to realize their full identity as fathers. While moms usually were thoroughly in love with their babies the instant they appeared, it was not strange for it to take a few months for daddies to become smitten with them. Some kind of feedback—direct eye contact, a smile, or a giggle—was sometimes required for fathers to completely bond with baby, after which there was no turning back. The manliest of men could turn to mush hearing a single "Da da" and, years later, have no problem whatsoever wearing a princess tiara at a pretend tea party. "I'd always wondered if I could give up my life for someone else," said one new dad who went through such a transformation, convinced that "this is the kind of thing you learn about yourself when you become a father."[16]

The love and devotion most dads expressed toward their children led many researchers to believe that the behavioral patterns of fatherhood are rooted in biology. Men may have an innate paternal instinct, as studies indeed showed, but from an early age it was rarely encouraged or allowed to fully develop. Women, on the other hand, were often urged when they were children to nurture their maternal instinct, a distinction that played out later in life. "Moms are schooled on the baby business from the moment they're given a doll to hug and hold," explained Geoff Williams in *Baby Talk* in 2003, "but my memories of playing with a Han Solo action figure never helped me when it came to taking care of my daughter." Fathers thus had to learn how to connect on a deep level with their infants, while mothers did not, general belief still held; the fact that women carried the fetus inside their bodies also naturally contributed to the thinking that maternal instinct was more powerful than the male equivalent.[17]

Against this backdrop, experts recommended that men undertake all kinds of activities—making a will, stopping smoking, painting the nursery, buying a stuffed animal—to jumpstart the connection between father and baby—all things considered unnecessary for women. Touching one's partner's belly to feel the fetus kick or talking (or even better singing) to him or her in utero were also ways men could establish a relationship with the baby before it was born, people like Greg Bishop, founder of Boot Camp for Dads, advised. To babies, "moms represent comfort and security [while] dads represent what's new and interesting," claimed Bishop, seeing fathers' main role at this stage as to "add adventure to the mix."[18]

For some soon-to-be dads, adventure was the last thing they wanted added to the mix of fatherhood. A surprising number of men had never changed, fed, or even held a baby, making their imminent experience as fathers all the more terrifying. For such men, Boot Camp for Dads offered a crash course in the art and science of fatherhood, and a way to gain literal hands-on experience with infants. Boot Camp for Dads put on workshops across the country, with veterans showing prospective fathers the ropes when it came to taking care of babies. Given the responsibilities of the new fatherhood, the program was long overdue; many men were expected to be an essential piece of the parental partnership but had no idea how to do so. Pregnant women were likely to actively seek information about childcare and were often plugged into a social network dedicated to such, but men typically did and were not, leaving them in the dark when it came to how to tend for a newborn. About 150,000 men had attended boot camp workshops in 250 locations since 1990 when the program began. In addition to providing the nuts and bolts, Boot Camp for Dads made baby care seem less threatening and even fun, smoothing the path to fatherhood.[19]

Most dads-to-be, however, had no need for a crash course in infant care, comfortable with the idea that they would learn on the job. Some new fathers quickly became experts in the field, so much so that moms found themselves in a kind of competition with them. Ayelet Waldman, for example, considered her husband to be "the perfect mom," envious of how the man skillfully tended to their baby, competently cleaned the house, and joyfully played with their three older kids, all without a peep of protest. Her husband was the "feminist's fantasy dad," she believed, simply better at childcare if such things could be measured in objective terms. While appreciative of her husband's efforts, Waldman also found the situation rather irritating, making her feel less of a parent. Although not especially enthusiastic about breastfeeding, Waldman was considering doing just that for their newborn as that was one thing her husband certainly could not do, giving her an edge in at least one aspect of parenting. "I want the absolute primacy that defines and accompanies the traditional role of mother," she wrote in *Parenting*, counterbalancing the more usual circumstances in which fathers felt they were playing second fiddle.[20]

Given how some other men found it difficult or impossible to adapt to the responsibilities of fatherhood, however, Waldman had little to complain about. A certain subset of men found themselves questioning their masculinity after becoming dads, seeing fatherhood as a form of domestication or, worse, subjugation. Despite the great strides men had made over the last couple of decades in adding more of a masculine component to parenting, there remained some confusion over the gender dynamics of fatherhood. Those coming from a more traditional point of view still saw parenting essentially as a feminine domain, meaning they had to sacrifice some of their manhood if they were to be good fathers. "I am man, hear me bleat," whined Fred Leebron in *Parenting* in 2004, one such man who did not understand that being a father was one of the most manly experiences to be had. Leebron admitted to always being either too nice or too mean in his fathering, seeing the former as a defining feminine characteristic and the latter as a distinctively masculine one. "Meanness" was for him a way to reassert his masculinity after having children, in other words, a strange and disturbing take on things. His masculinity robbed from marriage and fatherhood, Leebron was having a personality crisis, not knowing who he was anymore once his "manhood" was removed. Leebron's story was a sad one, particularly for his children, who were missing out on the benefits an authentically masculine figure typically brought to family life.[21]

A KIND OF EMOTIONAL JAZZ

At its best, fatherhood was not just an opportunity to express one's masculinity but the means to become a better human being. Those men who were most invested in fatherhood recognized that they, rather than just their kids, were gaining from the parental experience. Men (especially ex–"bad boy" celebrities) often credited fatherhood with saving them from an unhealthy lifestyle and self-destructive behavior; the responsibility of caring for another human being forced them to finally grow up and, most importantly, stay alive. (Fathers actually live longer than nonfathers, perhaps the most tangible, self-based reason to have a child.) Shifting the focus from oneself to others was another plus of becoming a dad, many reported, as was the realization of what was really important in life. Enthusiastic dads instinctively knew that the word *father* was not just a noun but a verb, believing the endeavor should be pursued consciously and deliberately. Providing for and spending time with one's kids was great but not quite enough, this line of thinking went; "fathering" implied an awareness of and objectivity to the parenting process itself, which was more likely to lead to a deep, emotional connection with a child.[22]

Men who had a child relatively late in life were most apt to be interested in the concept of fathering. There was little stigma attached to men in their fifties and sixties having children with significantly younger women, part of the increasing diversification of fatherhood. Older baby boomers perhaps saw fatherhood as one more way to remain eternally young despite their chronological age. It was not that unusual to find men eligible for membership in AARP with young children, particularly among those who did not have to worry about the high cost of raising a child. David Letterman, Paul McCartney, and Larry King were public figures who had children late in life, their fame and success helping to put a positive spin on the apparent trend. In 2007, fifty-nine-year-old Donald Trump had a son, well after raising four children into their teens and twenties. The following year, Michael Douglas was sixty-three and had a seven- and four-year-old with his younger wife Catherine Zeta-Jones, who was in the prime of her acting career. "Mommy makes movies and Daddy makes pancakes," he told readers of *Newsweek*, describing his new gig as "the role of a life-time."[23] That same year, fifty-two-year-old Kevin Costner and his wife, Christine, were expecting their first baby; the actor already had three grown children from his first marriage. Like many midlifers, Costner felt a kind of urgency with regard to becoming a father again. "I won't be around to see as much of this one's life as I'll get to see of my older kids' lives," Costner told *Good Housekeeping*, explaining, "I really want to be there for every single moment that I can."[24] Some older fathers were understandably mistaken for grandfathers, even if the men were doing everything they could to fight off the signs of age. These fathers found themselves racing against time, wanting to stay healthy for as long as possible in order to see their children grow up and become indepen-dent adults.[25]

"Re-fathering" was an ideal way for men to establish a meaningful relationship with a child, as Martin Carnoy outlined in his book *Fathers of a Certain Age*. The term meant becoming a father again later in life than was typical, either after remarrying or when one's original partner was significantly younger. Besides not being as obsessed with their ca-reers as many young men were, older dads tended to be wiser and have more patience than their first time around with a child. "Before, I was always fighting it," said J. Allan Hobson, referring to his internal conflict between career and parenthood. Hobson, a seventy-three-year-old Har-vard professor whose children ranged from eleven to forty-five years old, was now finding fatherhood easy, not something usually heard from younger men (especially ones with twins). Hobson felt he never had enough time to be the parent he could have been with his older kids because of his demanding teaching job. "The second time around is entirely different because I've made my mark," he explained, proving his point by claiming to have read five Harry Potter books from start to finish to his eleven-year-old twin sons.[26]

Children of men who had "re-fathered" also appeared to benefit from the situation, something that made a lot of sense given the abun-dance of time that was devoted to them. There were other reasons why "second time around" kids had what can be considered a paternal ad-vantage. "These men are in the rare position to make amends for prior failings, do the things they wish they'd done the first time around, avoid old mistakes, make good on old promises, and know from experience just how quickly the whole thing is over," wrote Marc Parent in describing his personal experience with his dad who had re-fathered. While Parent's father had been controlling and rigid with him—a byproduct of insecurity—he had become much more relaxed and patient by the time his much younger son was born. The elder Parent had also gained a greater ability to recognize the beauty in everyday things, making parenthood a happier affair for all parties involved a full generation later.[27]

Not just older men but those with a familiarity with Buddhist philosophy often made good fathers because they were capable of recognizing the beauty in everyday things. With the interest in all things Eastern over the last couple of decades, it is not surprising that Zen was seen as an element of good fathering. Hugh O'Neill, who wrote frequently about fatherhood in *Best Life*, saw being a dad as "a kind of emotional jazz," something that should be more improvisational than linear or rigid. Less clarity was better than more, he argued in 2007, wishing he had not tried to follow and enforce so many rules in raising his own kids. Likewise, "frazzle" was a normal part of family life, O'Neill felt, meaning parents should try to welcome it rather than attempt to get rid of it. Tall buildings and suspension bridges were designed to sway a bit, he pointed out, a good analogy for parenthood. "Embrace the uncertainty," O'Neill urged other men, thinking Buddha would have made a great dad.[28]

Sam Grobart, writing for the same magazine a year and a half later, also believed fathers could benefit from an acquaintance with Zen Buddhism. Fatherhood demanded one focus on what was important and ignore the rest, he explained, an idea that was very much consistent with Buddhist philosophy. As well, being single was all about "me-ness," he, like many others, noted, while becoming a dad for the first time left much less room for the self to run wild. The Zen Buddhist concept of *mu*, or "emptiness," was directly applicable to fatherhood, Grobart maintained, in that one had to shrink one's ego for the sake of another individual.[29]

Not at all Zen-like were those dads who viewed fatherhood as a sort of competition. Some men found themselves constantly carrying their toddlers around when they did not need to, for example, as a way to express their masculinity. (Strollers were seen as very un-macho among those men who felt their masculinity was threatened by becoming fathers.) For such competitive types, tossing children in the air was less a form of play than a display of strength, both to themselves and to other men. Playgrounds were an ideal setting for dads to show other dads who was the manlier man. Pushing little ones higher on a swing than that guy next to you offered a kind of rush to men who approached fatherhood as a sport, their own athletic days now over. "Some primal paternal instinct kicks in and we temporarily become a bit feral," explained Christopher Healy in *Parenting*, as he one day found his testosterone level rising when he was assigned childcare duty.[30] Given the competitive streak that ran through many men, it was not surprising that fathers tended not to be very good in situations where their child faced some sort of emotional difficulty. Men were and are famously averse to psychology, very generally speaking, thinking that getting professional help in that regard was and is a sign of weakness or unnecessary. Unfortunately, fathers have been prone to apply their fear or distrust of psychology to their kids, seeing emotional problems simply as bad behavior versus an outcome of mental illness.[31]

The not very healthy idea of fatherhood as competition has also served as a visible part of consumer culture. In recent years, dads have shown considerable interest in all the gear that goes along with raising kids, something marketers have eagerly capitalized on. Jeep has licensed its brand to a maker of strollers, for example, knowing that certain men would transfer their passion for simulated adventure to pushing children around the local park in something that suggested ruggedness. Men have also been known to invite houseguests into their garages in order to proudly show off their fleet of strollers as if they were sports cars. (Some families have no less than four strollers for a single child—one designated "all-purpose," one for shopping, another for "off-roading," and one for jogging or rollerblading.) Needless to say, competitive or brand-conscious fathering has little or nothing to do with what is usually accepted as the true goal of parenting—establishing a deep emotional connection with a child.[32]

WHAT MATTERS TO MOMS

Besides being irrelevant to the essence of parenting, gear targeted to dads, no matter how cool, could not make them equal to moms in terms of public perception. Even seemingly minor cases of slighting or exclusion in parental matters were viewed by some as demonstrations of partiality toward mothers. Fathers-to-be were typically not invited to baby showers, for example, something that could be perceived as an early sign of maternal favoritism. "The baby shower is like the kickoff to the parenting game," objected Geoff Williams after he was not asked to be part of the party circuit organized for his pregnant wife. Williams, writing for *Baby Talk* in 2006, was so perturbed about the situation that he threw baby showers for "expectant dads," an idea that he thought would gain traction. Not surprisingly, Williams put a male twist on the tradition, serving up beer, deep-dish pizza, and chicken wings to his buddies while they watched ESPN or played Nintendo.[33]

While men being left out of baby showers may have been a trivial (and, for many, welcome) thing, there were larger indications that parenting still had not achieved gender equality. Corporate America had always treated women unfairly (it still disfavors mothers who leave work early), but a decent argument could be made that companies were now less sympathetic to fathers than mothers. Mothers leaving work early to take care of children was often viewed by work colleagues as a good example of "family values" in action and a rather heroic attempt to balance one's professional and personal life. Fathers doing the same was frequently viewed more critically by colleagues, however, a case in which the men were likely not doing a great job either at work or at home. A half century after its zenith, the postwar breadwinner model of fatherhood had not completely gone away, leaving some men feeling as if they had no chance of realizing the work–family balance they so eagerly sought. Men were confronting a similar kind of workplace discrimination and existential quandary that women had for decades, a predicament that few could have predicted in the 1950s.[34]

Already torn between two powerful drives—achieving "success" in their careers and spending time with their children at home—men confronted additional obstacles to achieving balance in their lives. Politicians left and right promoted "family values," but employers and society at large often seemed to support the philosophy more in theory than in practice. "For all the rhetoric about the benefits of fathers who are 'there' for their kids," wrote Eve Heyn in *Parenting* in 2003, "it can still be tough for a dad even to make it home for dinner." Leaving the job early enough to tuck one's kids in bed, leaving at five o'clock to pick them up at school, or working a couple of days a week at home to give mom a break could all be career suicide at some companies. More generally, there was a fine line between "heroic" expressions of father-hood, such as missing an important meeting to take a daughter to the doctor or volunteering to coach a son's baseball team on weekends, and being considered an undependable employee. Emergencies were one thing and completely understandable, in other words, but routinely putting kids ahead of work was quite another.[35]

Urged by society to be better parents, fathers thus felt frustrated when they made attempts to do so. Many dads wanted to be more involved with their kids and make a greater contribution to running the household but realized they were swimming upstream in their efforts. No one wanted to be labeled a "clock-watcher," especially at companies where one was expected to always be on the job if necessary. (Cell-phones, email, and texting had of course blurred the lines between personal and professional lives.) More companies were offering part-time, flextime, job sharing, telecommuting, or a week of extended work-days exchanged for one day off, but, for the most part, corporate Ameri-ca still held the view that, as the expression went, "time is money." Being seen as not pulling one's weight was heading into dangerous waters, stirring up resentment by making colleagues feel they had to work harder and longer. In a corporate culture reciting the mantra that "There is no 'I' in the word Team," nothing put one in the doghouse faster than the perception that one was shirking responsibilities or be-ing disloyal. Consequences of being seen as not fully committed to one's job could range from not getting a deserved promotion to being treated poorly by fellow employees to outright discrimination.[36]

Fathers themselves were also responsible for sabotaging their best-laid plans of putting family first. Within the professional world, size mattered to many men, whether that meant hours worked, one's title, or the literal bottom line, salary. Changing that perspective was not easy, especially for those men raised in a climate prescribing more traditional gender roles. For A-types especially, accepting the idea of not giving 100 percent at work was a major hurdle, as was the notion of playing merely a supportive role in family life. Still, many fathers were determined to find a solution to the work–home equation, whether on a formal or informal basis. Changing to a less time- or travel-intensive job, moving from the private sector to a government position, arranging for a four-day workweek (at 80 percent salary), getting to one's desk extra early, or moving closer to the employer to cut down on commuting were all things dads did to try to resolve the work-versus-home dilemma.[37]

The push-pull between work and home that many fathers experienced, combined with a wobbly job climate in the mid-2000s, was at times so stressful that it was keeping psychiatrists quite busy with male patients. Men in their thirties and forties were supposed to be hitting their career strides, but companies were looking to save money wherever possible, adding to the pressures of the American dad. Twentysomethings, many of whom had significantly more advanced technology skills, were nipping at these men's heels, another source of concern. Some men felt like they could not win at home either, never quite meeting their wives' high expectations. Things were certainly better for men than a decade earlier, when economic and social forces converged to give rise to the so-called angry white male, but many fathers were convinced they received less recognition and respect than they deserved. From a purely linguistic sense, mothers did appear to be more multidimensional than fathers, a reflection perhaps of their higher social status. Unlike the various types of moms (working, single, super, soccer, etc.) said to populate the country, "the title of dad has rarely been linked to a modifier," Michele Orecklin observed in *Time* in 2004. The "NASCAR dad," a reference to white, middle-aged, and working- or lower middle-class fathers, was an exception, but this label could not be said to do men any favors.[38]

Because they were so firmly entrenched in society, traditional gender stereotypes were hard to shake for both mothers and fathers. For the latter, the "Mr. Mom" image was particularly persistent, especially within popular culture. In 2007, for example, Martha Stewart hosted a "Mr. Mom Show" on her television program to celebrate National Men Make Dinner Day, each event sexist and insulting, according to Brian Braiker of *Newsweek*. Braiker, who took paternity leave for a full year after his daughter Freya was born, thought the idea of "Mr. Mom" was dated and not very funny even when the movie that spawned the term was released more than twenty years earlier. (The same could have been said of the 1987 *Three Men and a Baby*, in which a trio of guys discover the frustrations and joys of caring for an infant left on their doorstep. The Three Stooges had covered the same territory about forty years earlier.) As well, the notion of men making dinner one day a year was equally absurd, as even those not considering themselves part of "the new fatherhood" found themselves cooking up macaroni and cheese for their kids' supper every once in a while. Even *Parenting*, one of the new magazines dedicated to progressive fathering, had the phrase "What Matters to Moms" under the title of its covers, as if parenting did not matter to dads. (To be fair, men were famously known to ignore any and all parenting books and magazines, presumably for the same pride-related reasons they refused to ask for directions when lost.)[39] Still, fathers like Braiker did not want to be compared to mothers. "Don't call me Mr. Mom," he griped, thinking America had yet to give dads the full recognition or appreciation they justly deserved.[40]

THE MOST POWERFUL IDEA

That fathers were awarded anything less than equal status as parents was all the more unjustified given their preeminent role in literature throughout history. "Fatherhood is the most powerful idea in the history of ideas," Hugh O'Neill boldly declared in *Best Life* in 2007, citing the Bible, Homer's *Odyssey*, Sophocles's *Oedipus Rex*, Shakespeare's *King Lear* and *Hamlet*, Twain's *Adventures of Huckleberry Finn*, and all of Eugene O'Neill's works as evidence of such a provocative claim. Even what was arguably the most popular movie of all time, *Star Wars*, used fatherhood as its central plot device, another example of the potency of paternity within the arts. The Judeo-Christian religions were also much about fathers, O'Neill continued, with followers looking to God much like a traditional paternal figure—stern and judgmental while at the same time loving and forgiving. "We look to both Dad and the Deity for a sense of who we are and for our marching orders going forward," he observed, something that suggested a sense of awe should be attached to fatherhood rather than pity. Adding to the cultural and social weight of fatherhood was the simple fact that everybody had had one, at least biologically. Given that, fatherhood was not just about "fathering" but to have been "fathered"; it was, one could say, a two-way versus one-way street. Relationships between a father and child were thus multigenerational, adding to the complexity and depth of the subject.[41]

The universality of fatherhood, as well as most men's enthusiasm upon becoming a dad, made voices questioning the merits of paternity all the more striking. In 2007, author Michael Finkel continued in the tradition of *Esquire* writer Harry Stein who had riskily admitted his ambivalence about fatherhood twenty-some years earlier. Finkel went even further than did Stein, confessing in his book *Blindsided by a Diaper* that "this whole baby thing might have been a mistake." Many men soon after becoming a father reported how they had never experienced such love for another human being, but this was not the case at all for Finkel. "I was happier when I didn't have a child," he declared, knowing that saying such a thing was socially taboo, maybe even illegal. An odd thing about Finkel's predicament was that he had always wanted to have a kid, perhaps even more than his wife, making the reality of it all the more distressing. While he loved his daughter and believed that fatherhood had in some way enhanced his life, protecting her had become his new priority, completely wiping out his former independence and freedom. His self-oriented, hedonistic ways had disappeared with the arrival of the baby, raising the question of how many other men felt similarly but would never say as much. Still, Finkel and his wife were expecting a second child when his book was published, making one think that even for him the positives of fatherhood somehow outweighed the negatives.[42]

One has to wonder how Finkel was doing a few months later given the often conflicted feelings attached to having a second child. Like many fathers before him, Andrew Postman was concerned whether he could ever love his second child as much as his first. "Not only is it impossible for me to imagine being overwhelmed twice," he wrote in *Parenting* shortly before his son would be born, "but I also fear that the love for the second child will be somehow tainted because it'll be comparative whereas the love for the first one was and is pure." And because he already had childcare responsibilities, Postman had less time to prepare for a second, adding to his anxiety. In the days after his second child was born, Postman found himself ignoring the baby, his fears realized. Postman described the attention he had paid to his first child as "an unscattered beam," something impossible for the second simply because of the first. Ten weeks later, however, Postman had found resolution, appreciating the differences between his two children. "Love, this time around, has snuck up on me," he declared, a happy ending to the story. [43]

Regardless of how many kids one had, the positives of fatherhood for children were clearer than ever, research showed. For two or three decades now, study after study revealed that actively involved dads were instrumental in helping their kids grow up to be mature, resilient adults. Children benefited in a number of important ways from having a committed father around, according to the latest research. More emotional stability, better social skills, and a more positive worldview were attributed to kids whose dads sent a lot of love their way, psychologists had found, with just the reverse for fathers who were not around. [44] "Kids with involved dads are happier, more confident, and more independent," said Armin Brott, whose most recent book was *Fathering Your School-Age Child*. Studies indicated that kids with active fathers also got better grades in school and were more likely to attend college. [45] It was debatable whether the current obsession with puffing up a child's self-esteem was a good thing, but there was now a mountain of evidence suggesting that dads did just that.

Research documenting the significant contributions fathers made to child development further illustrated how dads differed from moms as parents. One study published in the *Journal of Applied Developmental Psychology* in 2009, for example, showed that fathers had a greater impact on young children's language abilities than mothers, proving once and for all that dads were much more than good play buddies. [46] Anecdotal evidence also suggested that fathers had a different operating system than mothers in terms of childcare. Men leaned toward making decisions themselves, while it was not unusual for women to consult with friends and even strangers before choosing a course of action. "Nowhere are men's and women's hunter-gatherer differences more apparent than in parenting matters," bemoaned Glen Freyer in *Parenting*, his own experience supporting his claim. While he, as the hunter, made decisions alone and quickly, his wife, as gatherer, collected as much information from as many people as possible. Freyer thus felt as if he was, as he put it, "married to the mob," always having to defend his opinions against those of a committee. [47]

Hard research and personal stories confirming the positive influence of fathers countered the argument some made that any kind of parental love, rather than a particular makeup of a family, was all that a child truly needed. A single mom or two moms were just as good as the mother-father structure, according to this view, implying that nurturance had no real basis in gender differences. Stephan Poulter, author of *The Father Factor: How Your Father's Legacy Impacts Your Career*, strongly disagreed with the "love" thesis, believing that fathers were essential for a child's well-being, both psychologically and socially. This was especially true for daughters, he felt. Because a father was typically the first man a girl loved, Poulter explained, their relationship served as a template for how she would relate to men throughout her life. Interestingly, Poulter believed the new fatherhood was largely smoke and mirrors; baby boomer dads were not all that different from the postwar father figure despite all the hoopla surrounding the former, he claimed. Today's fathers remained on the periphery of their children's emotional lives, Poulter argued, serving as good providers but rarely making a deep connection with them. Dads should not fall into the common trap of trying to be their child's "best friend," however, as parenting was a very different thing than friendship. Not surprisingly, Poulter considered a child's teen years the most challenging for each party, making it especially important for fathers to stay involved as much as possible.[48]

PROUD PAPAS

With more studies documenting the benefits of male parenting, much attention remained focused on the African American community, where absentee fatherhood was now rampant. About half of black children lived in fatherless homes, according to the latest studies, an alarming statistic that community leaders were trying to reverse. Bill Cosby was on a personal mission to confront the issue head-on, speaking to large crowds of African American men across the country and urging them to be better fathers. Although there was certainly a major problem, many were left with the impression that positive examples of fatherhood did not exist in the African American community, something obviously not true. (The parade of paternity tests of black men on daytime talk shows like *Maury* popularized the false belief that the vast majority of African American fathers had abandoned their families.)[49]

Some, however, were doing what they could to better reflect reality. A memoir, Ta-Nehisi Coates's *The Beautiful Struggle*, as well as a pair of photo-essay books, Carol Ross's *Pop* and Rachel Vassel's *Daughters of Men*, featured real-life accounts of loving black fathers, while the 2006 based-on-a-true-story movie *The Pursuit of Happyness* was about a single, temporarily homeless dad (played by Will Smith) going to extraordinary measures to provide for his son. (Smith's real-life son Jaden played the eleven-year-old boy, adding to the film's "fatherliness.") While Cliff Huxtable was not a very realistic depiction of a black (or white, for that matter) father, neither was the perpetually deadbeat dad often seen in popular culture, these stories reminded us.[50]

While black dads were not represented fairly by the media and fathers in general felt like they were largely forgotten or neglected, there was no shortage of media dedicated to parenting as a whole. Besides new magazines like *Parenting*, *Best Life*, and *Baby Talk*, the 2000s saw an explosion of parenthood-related shows on television, many of them based in the so-called "reality" genre. With a predominantly female viewership, TLC leaned decidedly toward motherhood and babies, offering shows such as *A Baby Story*, *Bringing Home Baby*, and *Surviving Motherhood*; the Discovery Health Channel also featured mommies and little ones, with shows like *Babies: Special Delivery*, *House of Babies*, *Birth Day*, *Runway Moms* (about expectant models), and something with the unfortunate name of *Yummy Mummy*.[51]

One could find fathers on *Supernanny* and *Nanny 911*, however, each of these shows featuring professional childcare givers who let parents know how well (or more often not well) they were doing.[52] Dads remained a staple on sitcoms, of course, serving in some fashion as role models for real-life ones. In 2008, *Parenting* asked moms which televisual fathers most resembled their husbands, the findings shedding a little light on the state of the American dad. Half of the mothers reported that their husbands were most like the involved-but-slightly-anxious Alan Harper role played by Jon Cryer in *Two and a Half Men*; 38 percent believed the good-provider-but-somewhat-sloppy Ray Barone (Ray Romano) in *Everybody Loves Raymond* was the closest match; and, more than a bit disturbingly, 12 percent said they were married to someone like the dumb-as-a-box-of-hammers-but-lovable Homer Simpson.[53]

In addition to *The Simpsons*, popular television shows in the 2000s included *The Sopranos*, *Californication*, *Family Guy*, and *American Dad*, all featuring unapologetically masculine, often complex fathers. Despite their many flaws and foibles, however, the men in the shows embraced their responsibilities as dads, reinforcing the prevailing view that fatherhood was indeed the role of a lifetime. The shows also supported the healthy, very real fact that American dads were a diverse lot, and it was only their ability to father that truly mattered. While it was worrying that one out of every eight American dads was cut from the same cloth as the thankfully fictional Homer Simpson, it was actual fathers drawn from popular culture who on the surface presented a larger concern. Reality shows such as *The Osbournes*, *Gene Simmons' Family Jewels*, and *Snoop Dogg's Father Hood* starred celebrities whose lifestyles suggested they would not make adequate much less good dads. Even in these often outrageous shows, however, fatherhood was typically portrayed as a unique and challenging but ultimately rewarding experience grounded in good old parental love.

Not surprisingly, the media continued their now two-decade-old lovefest with celebrity dads. A host of famous men including Kevin Bacon, Jeff Bridges, Andy Garcia, Tim McGraw, Harry Connick Jr., Benjamin Bratt, Matthew Broderick, Noah Wylie, Richard Gere, Will Smith, Howie Long, Billy Ray Cyrus, Adam Sandler, Jack Black, Matt Damon, Heath Ledger, Tobey Maguire, Seal, Jon Bon Jovi, Rod Stewart, Lionel Richie, David Duchovny, George Lopez, and John Travolta were featured in magazines for being, as *People* put it, "proud papas" or "top pops." (Bad fathers too were sometimes nominated by the media; Michael Lohan, David Hasselhoff, Eliott Spitzer, Woody Allen, and Ryan O'Neal were among *Best Life*'s 2008 list of ten worst fatherhood role models.)[54] Asking an individual to describe his or her relationship with a dad who had been famous was another way to approach celebrity fatherhood. (Children of Frank Sinatra, Hunter S. Thompson, and Gerald Ford did just that for *Best Life* in 2008.)

While stories about "top pops" were almost always fluff pieces purely designed to enhance a star's image, useful tidbits related to fatherhood could sometimes be gleaned from such articles. It was interesting to learn, for example, that Paul Bettany and his wife, Jennifer Connelly, rotated childcare duties and their respective acting careers on an annual basis. One year Bettany would make movies while Connelly spent time with their kids, in other words, with the situation reversed the following year and so on. Although few people could take advantage of such a schedule, the couple seemed to find an ideal balance between work and family life, something that could perhaps be adapted for regular folks.[55]

In fact, some divorced couples had through necessity formulated a parenting style that in some ways resembled that of the famous pair. Two-parent families were great, such ex-couples admitted, but single parenting was more efficient and offered some advantages over the traditional dualistic model, they held. Rather than do family activities together, as many couples did, more could get done when parents acted independently, this line of thinking went, a key advantage in our time-crunched society. Not only that, but children were effectively forced to take more responsibility when only one parent was around at the time, helping them become more self-sufficient. Given all the children of divorced couples, was the widely praised two-parent, "nuclear" family overrated, one had to wonder?[56]

DADS ARE DUDES

Possibly so, but that did not stop dads who spent relatively little time with their kids between Monday and Friday from going on a familial binge on weekends. "Weekend dads," that is, fathers who held nine-to-five (and sometimes plus) jobs during the week, frequently overdid it with young kids when it was their turn to take care of them on Saturday or Sunday. (Such dads were still married, unlike the divorced "weekend fathers" of the 1970s.) The trouble typically began innocently enough with a long stroll, after which fathers would gradually add more activities to the mix in an attempt to keep children increasingly entertained. Soon dads were heading to playgrounds, libraries, and bookstores with kids in tow on weekends, after which zoos, museums, and amusement parks became part of daily schedules. At some point the effort would hit critical mass (surprisingly often at Chuck E. Cheese, the often frenzied pizza/entertainment chain), with both fathers and children physically exhausted and weary of finding something new and exciting to do. The team would then happily settle in to simpler, home-based activities like cooking something up in the kitchen, everyone realizing that it was togetherness that counted rather than thrills.[57]

Whether or not one was a "weekend dad," fathers were spending more time with their kids than they used to. The average father devoted roughly seven hours per week to "primary child care" in 2009, one study found, which was twice as much time as in 1965. Of course, fatherhood had changed not just quantitatively over the decades but qualitatively. A new kind of parenting book had recently appeared on bookshelves, notably, written by men who investigated their role as fathers as if they were exploring any other subject. Michael Lewis's *Home Game* and Sam Apple's *American Parent: My Strange and Surprising Adventures in Modern Babyland* were two such books, each more in the spirit of Malcolm Gladwell's *The Tipping Point* than your typical parenting how-to. Nancy Gibbs of *Time* believed that men in general had an engaged-but-relaxed approach to parenting, something that women should appreciate and even learn from. (Research showed that mothers often acted as gatekeepers of childcare, either encouraging or discouraging their partners from active involvement in parenting, meaning they still "called the shots" in many if not most families.)[58] In short, fathers were acting like men instead of trying to emulate their female partners. "Dads are dudes," she observed, thinking the current interpretation of masculinity was well suited for raising children.[59]

With men now free to emphasize their masculinity in fathering rather than having to repress it, the differences between moms' and dads' respective parenting styles were sometimes startling. Even wives were taken aback by their husbands' bull-in-a-china-shop parenting tactics but, more often than not, surprised by how effective they were. Tantrums could be easily resolved by simply slinging the child over one's shoulder like a sack of potatoes, some dads had discovered, not a maneuver most mothers would consider, much less attempt. It took plenty of effort for moms not to think their partners' parenting style was "wrong" and to resist thinking that they should do things precisely the way they did. "His way often works just as well as mine—if not better," admitted Emily Bloch in *Parenting*, coming to see that difference, rather than right and wrong, defined their approach to childcare. Bloch advised other moms to accept dads' inclination to put their kids in seemingly risky physical situations, routinely ignore details, and occasionally act like children themselves. Allowing for more flexibility and improvisation in schedules was another area she suggested mothers tolerate if not embrace, knowing that fathers were less likely to force their kid to do something simply because it was on the calendar.[60]

Some moms, however, were not so sure, thinking that men's seeming inability to follow schedules, incapacity to take direction, proneness to inattention, expectations for constant praise for their contributions, and, the old standby, overly rough way of playing with kids, made them less than ideal parents.[61] Even mothers who considered their mates to be "more dedicated than any father I know" were reluctant to delegate more childcare responsibilities to them, fearing the worst. That was the case for *Newsweek* writer Lorraine Ali, who, like most moms, was not happy to be spending twice as many hours as her partner (fourteen versus seven per week) in taking care of their kids. Ali's husband was allegedly clueless about how to properly feed or dress their child, and he reportedly had little idea of where their son's favorite toys were located. Enrolling their kid in summer camp was completely beyond his powers, she believed, leaving all activity scheduling up to her. "The 'new dad'? Give me a break," Ali spouted, tired of hearing about the au courant more involved type of fatherhood when she did most of the parenting.[62]

While women debated the merits of men as parents, dads continued to voice their protest over how they deserved more credit than they received. Fathers' taking care of their children was still sometimes referred to as "babysitting," for example, something not so for mothers. Shawn Bean was one dad who found the word offensive but was not too surprised when the "B" word came up, given the verb-related definitions of "mother" and "father" in the *Oxford American Dictionary*. "Mother" was "to bring up a child with care and attention," he pointed out, while "father" was "to treat with the protective care usually associated with a father." While the value of mothering was expressed in absolute or unqualified terms, in other words, the same could not be said to be true of fathering. Googling "mother" yielded millions more results than "father," Bean added, another sign that men were not parentally equal in the public's mind. "When it comes to parenting, Mom is CEO, Dad is Regional Assistant Director of Operations," he quipped, not optimistic that that perception would change anytime soon given how deep-seated it was.[63]

In his 2009 book *Home Game*, Michael Lewis expressed much the same sentiment, thinking that nobody admired dads, not even their families. Fathers were doing much of the work of parenting but not getting much acknowledgment for it, the author of *Liar's Poker, Moneyball*, and other popular books argued in his latest one, a complete reversal of some critics' claim that dads got too much parental credit. "The American father of a baby is really just [considered to be] a second-string mother," Lewis wrote, believing that men had received little in return for the new paternal responsibilities they had taken on. Wives looked at their husbands as "unreliable employees," children preferred their mothers when things got tough, and Americans as a whole viewed fathers condescendingly, feeling sorry for them more than anything else. Lewis had three children of his own but clearly did not embrace the idea that fatherhood was the role of a lifetime. Men "got fleeced," he concluded, the parental deal they had struck with women over the last few decades a bad one.[64] More questions about the role of fathers in family life were about to be raised, however, as the American dad once again took a turn in a new direction.

5

MANNY KNOWS BEST

Wanted: Active Male Caregiver.
—Posting in Fordham University's student-employment office, 2010

The posting in Fordham University's student-employment office may have been considered odd or even salacious just a few years ago, but no longer. A twenty-year-old student applied for the position, interviewed with the family from SoHo, the fashionable Manhattan neighborhood, and was soon taking care of two young boys. The student had become a "manny," a male nanny, someone who is in increasing demand in big cities like New York and Chicago. (Britney Spears, Madonna, and Gwyneth Paltrow each reportedly employed mannies, adding to the hipness factor.) Such mannies (or "Gary Poppins") now represent about 10 percent of placements by childcare recruitment agencies in those cities, a number that is likely to grow as the stigma surrounding male caregivers lessens. (Sexual abuse understandably remains a concern, although some mannies are hired by wives who fear their husband may have an affair with a nanny.) A greater number of male applicants due to the 2007 to 2009 recession also partly explains the phenomenon, as college graduates with experience in education and social work explore relevant career alternatives. Some single moms, lesbian couples, and traditional families with boys, however, are specifically interested in hiring a manny. "They're looking for a positive male role model," explained Ingrid Kellaghan, CEO of the Cambridge Nanny Group in Chicago, in 2012, expecting to see more placements of mannies in the future.[1]

That men were being considered positive role models as caregivers to children—perhaps even more "positive" than women—illustrates how far fatherhood has come in American society. Not that long ago considered "the other parent," subservient in most respects in domestic matters to mothers, fathers have gained considerable social status based on the very real contributions they are making to family life. Fatherlessness has only worsened in recent years, however, lending a kind of schizophrenic or bipolar dimension to male parenting. Efforts to bridge this "father gap" are being made at all levels, but more should be done to reduce the number of fatherless households in this country. The reasons to do so are all the more justified given the growing amount of research proving that fathers are important, if not essential, to a child's long-term well-being. What might be called "fatherhood studies" is an emerging field as scholars from various disciplines approach the topic in order to add to our understanding of men and gender in general. The most exciting findings are coming from neuroscience, as researchers link fathers' brain chemistry to the ways they interact with their children. We are clearly on the threshold of a new era of fatherhood, as more "secrets" about the American dad are revealed.

THIS IS A WAR

The first decade of the twenty-first century proved to be a significant one for fatherhood in America, as more men embraced what they considered "the role of a lifetime." A key factor for the raising of dads' voices in the national conversation was that the most powerful man in the world—the President of the United States—was an unequivocally loud champion of fatherhood. In fact, one could argue that the most public confirmation of the importance of fatherhood in recent years came in a 2011 essay written by Barack Obama. Published exclusively in *People* magazine on Father's Day of that year, the piece was a prime example of how many fathers adopt a parenting style based on what was missing from, rather than present in, their own childhood. "I grew up without a father around," the president wrote, his dad having left the family when Barack was just two years old. The couple divorced the following year, and his father died in an automobile accident when Barack was twenty-one.[2]

Although Obama's mother and grandparents did a good job raising him and his sister, the absence of a male parent left an emotional wound that the fifty-three-year-old president still clearly felt. Obama made a conscious effort to be with his own children as much as possible despite choosing a profession that demanded he be away from home much of the time. (Eating dinner with his family was a particular priority, even when he was in the White House.) Time, both its quantity and quality, was at the heart of being a good father, he correctly believed, as was providing structure for a child. Obama also made a point of being actively involved in the everyday lives of his two daughters, including making sure they did their chores and homework. "Above all I've learned that children need our unconditional love," his essay concluded, this the most essential component of parenting.[3]

The fact that President Obama's own father was largely missing from his childhood gave him a personal stake in the issue of fatherless families. Obama mentioned the problem not only in the *People* essay and frequently in speeches but in his administration's policies, putting his words into action. The president was of course well aware that kids without dads around were much more likely to drop out of school, live in poverty, and commit crimes and end up in prison, realities that supported the funding of father-related initiatives over the course of his eight years in office. While his predecessor, George W. Bush, focused on marriage in his own domestic policies, Obama concentrated on the fatherhood crisis, angering some conservatives in the process. The fact that the problem was especially bad within the African American community no doubt played a role in the president's decision.[4]

During his tenure (and previously as a United States senator), Obama established a variety of "responsible fatherhood" programs, following through on his 2009 Fatherhood and Healthy Families Taskforce and his Fatherhood and Mentoring Initiative established the following year.[5] The latter hosted community forums on fatherhood and "personal responsibility" around the country, and organizations affiliated with the initiative sent out e-newsletters "featuring articles, tips and resources from prominent leaders in the fatherhood and family fields and information about model programs."[6]

President Obama's concerted efforts to improve the state of fatherhood in the United States endure, as a visitor to Fatherhood.gov will testify. The website is sponsored by the National Responsible Fatherhood Clearinghouse (NRFC), a national resource funded by the Office of Family Assistance (OFA). Through Fatherhood.gov and other avenues created during the Obama administration, the NRFC provides research and strategies for men to be better dads by becoming more involved in their children's lives. The site also offers a "Responsible Fatherhood Toolkit" for those who want to start programs in their own local community that help dads "get and stay on track," as the website states. One can also take President Obama's "Fatherhood Pledge," which goes:

> I pledge to renew my commitment to family and community;
>
> I recognize the positive impact that fathers, mothers, mentors, and other responsible adults can have on our children and youth, and pledge to do all I can to provide children in my home and throughout my community the encouragement and support they need to fulfill their potential.[7]

As he hoped it would, Obama's national appeal for fathers has trickled down to local communities. One very big community—New York City—even appointed a fatherhood "czar" to find ways to get low-income dads more involved in their children's lives. Well aware of how problematic fatherlessness was in that city, Mayor Bloomberg named Alan Farrell head of the city's new Fatherhood Services agency in June 2010. (One-third of the children in the five boroughs had no father around, with an astounding 54 percent rate in the city's African American community and 42 percent rate in the Latino community.) Farrell's resume was highly impressive, but an important consideration was that he had himself grown up without a dad, giving him a personal connection to the job. While the program's stated intent was to improve the well-being of kids by encouraging fathers to stick around, its more practical, long-term goal was to reduce the city's crime rate and jail population. In addition to the emotional cost, fatherlessness had major economic consequences, incentivizing elected officials to invest in programs to fight it.[8]

Community leaders in other cities around the country are doing what they can to stem the tide of fatherlessness. David Hirsch, founder of the Illinois Fatherhood Initiative and CEO (chief encouragement officer) of TEAMDAD ("a social business venture whose primary purpose is to create social impact by promoting responsible fathering and connecting fathers and children," its website states), clearly understands that reducing fatherlessness requires fighting back. "This is a war," he asserted, convinced that, "we have to win it." Hirsch estimated that twenty-four million American kids were being raised in homes without dads, meaning the nation's fatherlessness rate was about 40 percent (significantly higher than the 25 percent other experts cited). Hirsch cited four main causes for fathers' absenteeism: one, paternity not being established at a child's birth, meaning there was no dad to begin with except in a biological sense; two, the high rate (41 percent) of births to unwed mothers, suggesting that marriage was highly correlated with fatherhood; three, the high rate (about 50 percent) of divorce; and four, most distressingly, the simple lack of interest among many men to be fully (or even partially) involved with their families. A large part of an entire generation of children was growing up without a dad, Hirsch correctly pointed out, with the social costs all too clear. Interestingly, Hirsch deviated from political leaders in believing that community programs were not the solution to the problem. The war had to be fought on an individual level, he maintained, with each man required to make a personal commitment to his family. "We have the resources to win this war," Hirsch confidently concluded, while at the same time wondering if we had the necessary resolve and conviction.[9]

DO FATHERS MATTER?

Alongside this official recognition of the value of fathers, however, has sprung an intensifying counterargument that they are less necessary than commonly believed. In a 2010 article in the *Journal of Marriage and Family*, Judith Stacey and Timothy Biblarz pointed out that much of the data supporting the idea that fathers are vital is flawed. All kinds of variables go into the parenting equation, making any assessment of "father" or "no father" in a family overly simplistic. As others had previously suggested, it is the quality of parenting rather than the number of parents or their gender that really matters, Stacey, a professor at New York University, and Biblarz, who taught at the University of Southern California, argued. "The bad news for Dad is that despite common perception, there's nothing objectively essential about his contribution," agreed Pamela Paul, author of *Parenting, Inc.*, challenging the generally accepted notion that fathers are an indispensable component of family life.[10] For people like Paul, men's increasing irrelevance when it came to parenting parallels their overall social and economic decline in the United States, as women have caught up to or surpassed them in income, education, and other key factors.[11]

Many disagreed with such a conclusion, however, none more so perhaps than science journalist Paul Raeburn. In his 2014 book *Do Fathers Matter?*, Raeburn provided a heap of evidence supporting the view that male parents were indeed an integral part of family life. The historical focus on mothers as parental figure has obscured the role of fathers, he pointed out, making it appear that the latter were generally bystanders except for their breadwinning capacity. Newer research from a cross section of disciplines including psychology, sociology, biology, and even neuroscience has, however, reshaped our understanding of the kinetics of families and children. From conception on, fathers have a direct impact on the physical, intellectual, and emotional well-being of their children, Raeburn argued, sometimes in surprising ways. A father simply being present during the mother's pregnancy leads to healthier babies, rather amazingly, implying that fetuses can somehow sense whether or not their biological father is nearby. Dads also serve to "bullyproof" their children (make them less likely to torment other kids) and help them acquire language (more so than moms), just a couple of other recent discoveries that demonstrate the major influence of fathers. Fathers matter a great deal, Raeburn and many scientists countered, suggesting that a male parent is quite different from a female one.[12]

Given many dads' more practical contributions to family life, many would agree they are truly vital. *Parenting* found that fathers are usually responsible for home and yard repair, car maintenance, and child discipline, all dirty jobs (sometimes literally so) that mothers are not particularly interested in doing. Dads also often take on the less attractive parenting and household duties, the magazine found, such as cleaning up a child's various bodily fluids when accidents occur in the house or car, getting rid of bugs and other critters, and plunging backed-up toilets, these too typically not on moms' priority list. While these are perhaps minor inconveniences compared to mothers' long list of responsibilities (not to mention the indescribably difficult job of having the baby in the first place), men do much to keep a household running, another plus for a traditional family setup.[13]

Others believed that while fathers are not completely expendable, they are receiving too much credit. Paul Scott of *Parents* made the very good point that many fathers are neither stay-at-home dads nor primary breadwinners, leaving them in a literal no-man's-land of responsibility. Such men "work a little and parent a little and likely spend a fair amount of time worrying about not doing so hot at either," he wrote in 2010, confessing that he was part of what he called "the new neither." Most men want to be more involved with their kids yet still look to their careers to satisfy their egos, making them fully committed to neither family nor work. Some also said they wanted to do more around the house but claimed their wives prevented them from doing so, thinking they just would not do a very good job. (As with childcare, men are known to approach housework in a different way than women, seeing routine chores as do-it-yourself projects requiring power tools and many trips to the hardware store.) Not surprisingly, given the technology available, a host of "daddy blogs" have sprung up on the Internet for fathers to vent their feelings about such issues with like-minded men. Writers for *Daddy Dialectic*, *Dadcentric*, *DadWagon*, *Dadtalk*, and *Dads and Daughters* all share the myriad experiences of fatherhood and offer useful advice, in the process building a stronger community of men.[14]

Daddy bloggers and their followers who are committed to all things fatherhood are also getting together at the Dad 2.0 Summit (a spin-off of the Mom 2.0 Summit). The annual conference, which began in 2012, is a beehive of bloggers on fatherhood, with marketers and social media people tagging along to plug into the online paternal scene. Attendees learn how to start a daddy blog or leverage one by partnering with marketers eager to reach a male audience, much like the female-oriented mommy blog phenomenon of a decade earlier. Sponsors of the conferences include Unilever's Dove Men+Care body care, a brand that has taken the lead in targeting the active, more involved father. "Men are more receptive to messages about taking care of themselves after they have children," Rob Candelino, vice president for marketing at Unilever, told the *New York Times*. Research shows that men are making more purchase decisions for their families, something not surprising given the greater responsibilities in general that they have taken on in recent years. (Marketers still typically refer to shoppers as "she," however.) Judging by the turnout for these events (about two hundred attendees), daddy blogging is apparently a big business, with money to be made by those who are skilled at equipping men with information dedicated to the art of fatherhood. "Society is ready for a new narrative about dads," observed Candelino, with marketers like him ready to craft that more realistic story.[15]

The idea that it was time for "a new narrative" about fatherhood was reflective of the vast transformation of the institution itself. "Archie Bunker is dead," declared Shawn Bean in *Parenting*, the iconic paternal figure of *All in the Family* (as well as the almost as unforgettable Al Bundy of *Married with Children*) thankfully no longer representative of the American dad in any real way. Bean also made the interesting observation that the word *dad* had at some point surpassed *father* in everyday conversation, a change in our linguistic habits that carries heavy semiotic weight. Darth Vader of *Star Wars* was, as he told his son Luke Skywalker, a "father" versus a "dad," he like Bunker and Bundy symbolic of a kind of paternal character who no longer possessed any significant amount of social currency. A host of markers related to fatherhood and, more broadly, American culture as a whole—male parents' responsibilities, men's dress codes, and nearly everyone's technological fluency—have all evolved, making the dad of the twenty-first century almost unrecognizable from the one of a few decades past.[16]

While experts argue over the relative value of fathers in family life, others make legitimate complaints about some after they have made their exit. Divorced dads who misrepresent the degree of involvement with their kids in social media have proven to be a particularly annoying concern to moms. Much to the dismay of their exes, men have taken to posting numerous photos of their children on Facebook to give the false impression that they are spending loads of time with them when that is simply not the case. Fathers have been known to extensively document seemingly happy times shared with their kids on visiting days, sometimes even staging shots or asking the kids to change clothes to make it appear that the photos were taken on different occasions. Moms with primary custody become infuriated when they see their ex-husband's Facebook page filled with photo-ops of their children, knowing that the presentation is a complete sham. Those men who have been lax about paying child support are especially prone to using social media as a publicity device to suggest they are, at the end of the day, good dads. Worse, perhaps, men also use the trick to make themselves appear more desirable to women, well aware that the image of an obviously caring, loving dad is powerful dating bait. [17]

A CONSTANT PROCESS OF REDEFINITION

One clear sign that fathers matter is what typically happens when they die. With millions of baby boomers now entering their sixties, the death of one's father has become a common topic of conversation and cause of concern. Many are not prepared to bid goodbye to their dad, a reflection of our death-phobic society. [18] Death memoirs in books and magazines have become a literary genre all their own as writers process the loss of a loved one, including their father, and the online universe is filled with remembrances of dads who recently passed away. In *Esquire* in 2012, for example, Mark Warren paid tribute to his recently deceased father by describing some of the more memorable words he used, including those spoken on his deathbed. [19] Another article by Stephen Marche in that same issue described how the author told his son that his grandfather had suddenly died, a painful task that many men must experience. [20] Such stories remind us that the concept of fatherhood is a two-way street, that is, that paternity encompasses not only caring for a child but also the relationship between oneself and a male parent.

In reflecting on his father's death and having to pass on the sad news to his son, Marche was especially qualified to assess the importance of fatherhood. "As masculinity continues to undergo a constant process of redefinition, fatherhood has never mattered more," he boldly maintained, a byproduct of the decline of patriarchy. The social power of the two other traditional symbols of masculinity—work and war—had over the centuries weakened as they became more gender neutral, leaving fatherhood as the principal sign of masculinity. Many men believe they became "men" when they became dads, Marche observed, serving as more evidence of the significance of fatherhood for gender identity. It is the obligations of fatherhood as well as the fact that it binds one to other people that accounts for both its appeal and cultural currency, he felt. Unless a man abandons his family, in other words, fatherhood usually functions as a strong link to at least one additional individual for the remainder of his life; this deep connection with another human serves as a path to a "fuller" male experience. Men desire to be dads and want to spend as much time as possible with their children because it is the sole remaining opportunity to demonstrate their masculinity to themselves and others, Marche concluded, a very interesting theory that deserves further exploration by researchers.[21]

The role of fatherhood in defining masculinity represents not just an intriguing sociological topic but can lead to important findings useful for the real world. Much of fatherhood as a field of study, in fact, requires further investigation if we are to find ways to persuade "truant" men to accept and even embrace their responsibilities to their families. It is well known that becoming a father changes men in certain areas of life, such as the desire to be healthier and more cautious. But the sheer quantity of research on fatherhood is relatively low, especially when compared to other aspects of family life. "In a world where the effects of motherhood are a source of scientific and cultural fascination, information on how fatherhood affects men, mentally and physically, is scarce," wrote Kim Painter of *USA Today*, with some obvious knowledge gaps (such as whether fathers are indeed healthier than non-fathers). Two-thirds of adult males in the United States are fathers, in fact, making the subject an important one by numbers alone.[22]

Thankfully, scholars are now giving more thought to effects of fatherhood on men and even to the "scientific" reasons why they want to become dads. "What explains men's desire to have children in the first place?" some are asking, theorizing that the urge to do so must be at least partly embedded in human biology. Evolution is also a likely contributing factor, as is the social and economic advantage to building generational wealth. And again, men having long-term relationships with families, (usually) women and children, appears to encourage positive behaviors like work and discourage risky and destructive ones.[23] Various governmental agencies, notably the National Institutes of Health, are pursuing scientific studies of fatherhood in order to improve the likely outcomes of children's lives. If more was known about what made good dads tick, the thinking goes, perhaps there are effective strategies to make more fathers commit to their families. Grants are being awarded and symposia held, with social scientists from a number of fields examining the relationships between dads and their children and drilling down to the fundamental activities of fathering—breeding, bonding, and providing. "We are only beginning to understand these relationships and more research is necessary to gain a clearer picture of how the relationship between children and their fathers affects men's health outcomes," wrote Tia L. Zeno and Robert M. Kaplan in the academic journal *Fathering*, the beginnings perhaps of a major field of study. [24]

Administrators at the University of Arizona also recognize the value of fatherhood as a scholarly discipline, offering what is likely the first college course in the subject. Hundreds of students at that university are attending the class, which explores the meaning of fatherhood for men and their families. This bodes well for the study of gender identity and relationships, an area that has historically tilted toward women. Rather than focus exclusively on American dads, however, the course at the Tucson campus cuts across many cultures and even species, approaching the subject from a very broad perspective. And rather than a how-to parenting class for students considering (or already pursuing) fatherhood, the class (titled "Men, Fatherhood, and Families: A Biocultural Perspective") is grounded in the social and behavioral sciences of psychology and anthropology. One key question the course asks is whether there are universal themes in human behavior when it comes to fatherhood, helping to put its expression in Western countries in valuable context. The interest in fatherhood among both governmental agencies and universities is a positive sign that promises to provide answers to the many remaining questions we have about men's decision to have children. Fatherhood is gradually coming out of the research shadows as more is understood about the complex roles men play in family life. [25]

THE NEW DAD

No team of researchers is doing a more thorough job of investigating the individual and social aspects of fatherhood than one at Boston College's Center for Work and Family. Since 2010, the team has on an annual basis been issuing fascinating studies related to fatherhood under the banner of "The New Dad," contributing immensely to the body of knowledge in what is becoming a legitimate field all its own.

That year, Brad Harrington and Fred Van Deusen of that institution along with Jamie Ladge of Northeastern University published the first of the series, "The New Dad: Exploring Fatherhood within a Career Context." The report presented the big idea that American men were leading "a quiet revolution," one steeped in the values of the "new fatherhood" movement that had been simmering for at least three decades at that point. With their initial study, the researchers went directly to one of the key issues of fatherhood—the complex dynamic between the dual responsibilities of worker and parent. "We are interested in the career identity and the paternal identity of new fathers and how the two roles integrate, conflict, and enrich one another," the authors put forth, using conversations with thirty-three men to better understand the relationship between breadwinner and caregiver.[26]

Not surprisingly, the trio confirmed in their research that fatherhood was acting as a prime catalyst for dads to construct their identity as men (just as Marche and others had theorized). "The men in our study were clearly re-thinking and re-defining traditional gender based roles," they reported, a reflection of the transformation of not just fatherhood but American culture in the twenty-first century. More specifically, the participants in the study saw themselves not just as providers but, ideally at least, equal partners in the taking care of children and home. And rather than view their careers as a vehicle to achieve success, men were more likely to see work as enabling a particular lifestyle for their family. Fatherhood was an opportunity for men to grow and mature as human beings, operating as an experience that encouraged the development of the desired attributes of patience, empathy, and understanding. Most compelling, perhaps, men considered themselves "whole persons" upon becoming fathers, the joys and challenges of looking out for another person leading to greater purpose and meaning in their lives. "Men seem poised to embrace a new definition of fatherhood and to step up to the challenges and the rewards of parenting in a much fuller sense than was the case in the past," the team concluded, adding that, "it is time we helped and encouraged them to do so."[27]

Having gained some interesting findings from their first, rather modest study, the team at Boston College expanded their exploration of contemporary fatherhood. (Beth Humberd of Boston College replaced Jamie Ladge as third researcher.) While the first study was based on qualitative research using a relatively small sample of interviews, the follow-up report published in 2011 relied on a quantitative survey of one thousand fathers. And rather than just talk to new dads, the team reached out to white-collar workers whose kids ranged from babies to teenagers. As with the initial study, the second revealed that American dads viewed fatherhood as the principal means by which to find fulfillment in life. Most respondents reported that they were happy with their jobs and wanted their careers to continue to advance, but just a small percentage (16 percent) of them said that work was their primary focus. Job security and flexibility were considered bigger priorities than moving up or making more money, a direct reflection of the men's desire to put family first. One of the central themes of masculinity—fathers' gradual shift from breadwinner to caregiver as a marker of identity—was borne out by the study, an important finding that paralleled anecdotal evidence. Although they desired to share parenting responsibilities equally with their partners, most men admitted they did not, however—another consistent theme in research related to fatherhood. It was easy for men to say they wanted to be more involved with their kids and contribute more to keeping the house running, but doing so was a much different story.[28]

The third report issued by the Boston College Center for Work and Family (with Iyar Mazar of the college replacing Beth Humberd as third researcher) focused on at-home dads. In their 2012 paper "The New Dad: Right at Home," the team explored in depth the issues around men who had left the workforce in order to be primary caregivers to their children. In talking to thirty-one men who did make such a leap, the researchers found that, contrary to popular belief, being a stay-at-home dad was usually a conscious choice rather than a response to losing one's job. As well, all types of men chose to become an at-home dad, dispelling the myth that only those with a strong, innate domestic streak made good primary caregivers to children.[29]

Despite volunteering for the position rather than being forced into it, becoming a stay-at-home dad was, needless to say, hardly easy, the Boston College team confirmed. Besides the long hours (sometimes as much as twelve a day), men often felt socially isolated and experienced a lack of respect from people who viewed their "job" as not much more than a glorified babysitter. This was unfortunate for a variety of reasons, including the fact that having an at-home, full-time parent allowed the other partner to flourish in her career. Not surprisingly, at-home dads made very good parents, the third study also reported, a function of the men's obvious devotion to and direct involvement with their children. Best of all, however, being a stay-at-home dad "increased the fundamental sense of meaning" in the lives of men who chose that path, the researchers again found, an affirmation of the very concept of fatherhood in terms of personal identity.[30]

In her own qualitative study with thirty-two stay-at-home dads, Catherine Richards Solomon has contributed additional valuable findings to an area where relatively little sociological research has been done. Solomon focused on how such men viewed their social status, publishing the results in *Fathering* in 2014. "Stay-at-home fathers enact fatherhood in ways that may be starting to transform traditional and new ideals of fatherhood," she wrote, pointing to both the increasing number of dads electing to be full-time parents and the ways they were taking care of their children as factors for the big changes taking place. Expectedly, just as the researchers at Boston College had determined, Solomon found that stay-at-home dads and their children shared an emotional closeness, the result no doubt of the kind of bonding that typically occurs in caregiving when a significant amount of time—both quantity and quality—is spent together.[31]

Unexpectedly, however, Solomon also discovered that the fathers she spoke with received positive reactions from others about their parental role and were widely recognized for doing important family work. Some male friends and strangers were envious of the full-time dads, wishing they could be (or, if older, could have been) in their place. "I feel a little bit like a rock star walking through downtown with a baby on my chest," said one of her subjects, contradicting the image of the neutered full-time father frequently portrayed in popular culture. From Solomon's study, at least, fathering appears to be "catching up" to breadwinning as a respected role for men, signaling a major cultural shift along gender lines. "Their [stay-at-home dads'] connection to their children was poignant and highlights how fatherhood, for some men, has evolved to one of intense engagement since the beginning of the 21st century," she concluded, hitting the nail on the head.[32]

The fourth in the series of reports issued by the Boston College Center for Work and Family was a valuable summary and analysis of the amazing body of knowledge it had amassed over the last three years. Published in 2013, "The New Dad: A Work (and Life) in Progress," took a deeper dive into the pool of qualitative research, drawing out further implications steeped in the "quiet revolution" men were leading. There was "a new, growing spirit of determination among men to fully embrace their roles as fathers," the team (with Jennifer Sabatini Fraone in place of Iyar Mazar as third contributor) posited, reiterating that the average American dad was significantly more engaged in family life than in the past.[33]

By investigating the social and cultural dynamics of fatherhood, Harrington, Van Deusen, and their colleagues did yeoman's work in expanding the field of gender studies, adding much to our understanding of men's relationships with their children, partners, and careers. What did the team get out of interviewing or surveying almost two thousand dads? "The portrait we paint is encouraging and enigmatic, promising and problematic," the trio stated, the huge strides made by men in taking on greater responsibilities within their families complemented by an array of challenges brought on by a more complex day-to-day existence. "Our work presents an image of male parents struggling with work-family conflict, but at the same time striving to be good workers, good fathers, and good men," they concluded, an excellent way to capture the rich pageant that is fatherhood in America today.[34]

BABY BJORNERS

The same conclusion would not be reached by anyone relying on the ways fatherhood has recently been presented in American popular culture. Many of today's dads grew up on 1980s sitcoms and are mightily disappointed by how fathers are now being portrayed on television. For every witty Cliff Huxtable from *The Cosby Show* and sympathetic Steve Keaton from *Family Ties*, there is a father whose role is clearly to play the fool. "These guys can barely muster the basic competency of Barney Rubble," thought Aaron Traister, unhappy about the distorted image of fathers on television even if the motivation was to entertain. "At a moment when American dads are more involved in family life than ever, I, for one, am not amused," he continued in *Redbook*, arguing that presenting fatherhood as emasculating was not just untrue but potentially damaging to the social identity of men. In shows such as *Up All Night*, *Modern Family*, *Parenthood*, *Guys with Kids*, *The New Normal*, and

Ben and Kate, fathers taking care of children are often made to appear ridiculous and, specifically, unmanly. Writers for these shows seemed to have been inspired by Raymond's less-than-confident character on *Everybody Loves Raymond* and, perhaps, the truly stupid Peter Griffin of *Family Guy*, a dubious ancestral heritage for paternity.[35]

Anyone enduring an extended session of contemporary television would indeed deduce that fatherhood has taken quite a tumble over the past few decades on that medium. In a handful of current shows, toting little ones in baby carriers is a common sight gag, visual shorthand that the male characters have been subjugated along gender lines. As well, fathers use babies to meet women in bars, keep tabs on old girlfriends, and as lucky charms at sports events, behavior that evoked the old stereotype that most men were less-than-responsible parents. There are exceptions, however. On *Louie*, a television show starring the comedian Louis C.K., the lead character never uses his daughters purely for comic relief, something producers of other programs could and should learn from.[36]

James Poniewozik of *Time* also wondered what was so funny about men on television taking care of babies, especially when the latter were literally attached to the former. For Poniewozik (like the dad who felt "a little bit like a rock star"), the ubiquitous baby carrier was not a sign of submission but rather a legitimate symbol of the value of the new kind of fatherhood that had flourished over the past generation. "Baby Bjorners," as he referred to men who strapped their infants to their chests, were likely to be deeply invested in parenthood, a wonderful and not humorous thing. Poniewozik added the new sitcom *Baby Daddy* to the list of father-unfriendly television shows and cited the movies *The Hangover* and *What to Expect When You're Expecting* as also paternally offensive. (A positive cinematic representation of fathers can be found in Michael Schwartz's documentary about Baltimore stay-at-home dads, fittingly titled *Happy SAHDs*.) The same was true of a recent Huggies commercial called "The Dad Test"; the spot made the claim that the brand of diapers and wipes were so easy to use that husbands did not require help from their wives. (Huggies dropped the commercial after numerous fathers complained.) Because the baby carrier mimics the profile of a pregnant woman, however, it was the prop of choice for those in the entertainment business to feminize men, a staple of sorts in comedy. Like Traister, Poniewozik concluded that the effect of such silliness was the very real impression that men were not naturally equipped to take care of children, something not at all true given all the evidence to the contrary.[37]

The poking of fun at fathers on television and in movies may seem harmless, but it appears to have serious, long-lasting effects. About 82 percent of fathers of young children believe there is an anti-dad prejudice in this country, a 2012 *Parenting* survey found, an unfair attitude given men's substantial contributions to family life.[38] One particularly unfortunate consequence of the negative portrayal of men as fathers in popular culture is that many dads believe the messages to be true. "Far too many of us buy into the myth that there are certain parts of parenting at which we are naturally incompetent," explained David Hill, author of *Dad to Dad: Parenting Like a Pro*, blaming not just the entertainment media but other men and family members for creating the misconception. With expectations low, some fathers viewed themselves as not very good nurturers, or simply inept at the basic task of childcare.[39]

Thankfully, there were reminders in the media that there were what Jill Herzig, editor-in-chief of *Redbook*, called "do-it-all dads." Her own husband not only met or exceeded the goal of many couples with kids—50 percent of parenting duties—but took on the kinds of responsibilities that men were famous for avoiding like the plague, such as arranging play dates, making doctor appointments, and finding a babysitter. "Somehow, in just one generation, men made a giant leap, and continue to evolve," she wrote, recalling that her own father was far more likely to disappear every Sunday than spend any time with her or her mother.[40] It was not surprising that the editor-in-chief of *Redbook* had such a happy story to tell about the progress of fatherhood. The magazine is a champion of American dads, finding them to be not just properly involved but the essence of masculinity. To prove its point, the magazine's website invites dads to submit pictures of themselves with their children, with the most attractive of the lot published. Its recent "Hot Dads with Babies" photo essay, for example, featured men from around the country (as well as British soccer superstar David Beckham) alongside their respective little ones, reinforcing the idea that fatherhood today can indeed be a testosterone-laden enterprise.[41]

Moms like Herzig appreciated having a "do-it-all dad," but some other women were less than pleased about having a man in the house who made it his mission to try to do it all. Being married to a man with seemingly endless energy and the need to control every parental moment was understandably a trying experience that left wives feeling they were merely onlookers in the family. New dads who consumed large quantities of parenting how-tos were especially prone to overdoing it, thinking of themselves as experts in all areas of raising a child, having read it in a book. Such dads were also predisposed to overprotecting children by checking, double-checking, and sometimes triple-checking any object that would come in contact with the kid. Overzealous fathers might also allow only immediate family members to babysit or even install video monitors in every room in the house where a child could possibly roam. A too involved dad was better than one who was absent, mothers in these situations agreed, but that was little compensation for the fact that their overbearing husband could at times drive them utterly crazy.[42]

As research studies have shown, most dads are not fanatical or try to do it all but do wish they could be more involved as fathers. Although they help out with housework and hold full-time jobs, these men still feel guilty about not spending more time with their children (and, paradoxically perhaps, not spending more time at work). As for mothers, the decades-long search for balance remains a major concern for fathers, as men continue to juggle the demands of work and family. Waking up in the middle of the night to do some work or staying at one's desk through lunch so that one can be home in time for dinner is not all that unusual. Missing a child's birthday, a soccer game, or the proverbial school play due to an out-of-town meeting can cause considerable stress, a reflection of the pressure men feel to be, as the T-shirt or coffee mug reads, "#1 Best Dad." The desire to be a better dad than the one they had as children is no doubt a contributing factor for contemporary fathers' conviction that they can always do and give more. Fathers today occasionally drop everything or play hooky from work to do something fun with their kids on a weekday afternoon, something their own dads would not even consider.[43]

Any time spent with one's child is a gift, most busy dads would say, but there is still something to be said for a little downtime. For always-on-the-go men, the demands of work and family have made the rare opportunity to be in the company of just oneself a rather cherished moment. Some men who used to dread a long commute to and from work are now, as fathers, relishing their alone or "me" time. Shawn Bean, who by 2011 was regularly writing about fatherhood for *Babytalk* magazine, was one such dad, seeing his more-than-one-hour drive each way to and from his office as a sanctuary from the storm of having an infant at home. "It's funny, everyone always talks about how moms need mom time," he observed, "but no one talks about whether dads need dad time." Fatherhood had changed dramatically over the past couple of generations, of course, but Bean's life was much like that of his father and grandfather when they went off to work to bring home the bacon for the family. For those who did not have the luxury, if one could call it that, of a long commute, Bean advised fathers of little ones to treat short, solitary periods of time in or out of the house as therapeutic retreats. The smallest of errands could serve as a much needed and deserved break from the responsibilities of taking care of a baby, he told readers, welcome news for new fathers wondering if they would ever have any real time alone again.[44]

AN INTERESTING TIME IN OUR CULTURAL HISTORY

While the producers of television shows and movies find a feminized father hilarious (or believe the audience will), there is at least one voice of reason in the media when it comes to the authentic masculine dad. Fatherhood and masculinity are equated in the pages of *Esquire*, argu-ably the most iconic voice of maleness in American popular culture. Alongside all the articles about swinging bachelor life are essays de-voted to some aspect of fathering, a clear indication that being a dad is hardly an exercise in femininity. "For a man, the relationship with his dad is the most formative of all relationships," wrote David Granger, editor-in-chief of *Esquire*, in explaining why the magazine regularly devotes pages to fathering. Quite simply, fathers teach boys how to be men, he maintained, regardless of how involved they are in their chil-dren's lives.[45] A 2012 issue of the magazine dedicated to fatherhood, for example, included an article on what to feed kids, instructions for leav-ing teenagers alone, a piece on how and when to start drinking with one's daughters, things fathers should teach sons, advice for dads with adult children, a style guide for fathers and sons, actress Mary-Louise Parker's remembrance of her dad, and, last but not least, a treatise on why not to have kids ("It's not a miracle, it's an epidemic," barked David Curcurito in his essay titled "Free as a Bird").[46]

Due much in part to Granger and his ethos of masculinity, men's magazines as a whole have led the way in recognizing the importance of fatherhood in American society. Deservedly known as "laddie" magazines a decade ago for featuring editorials to help young men be bad boys, the category has matured as its staff and ownership did. *Esquire* now considers fatherhood nothing short of a precious natural resource, seeing it as a cure for various social ills because of its direct correlation with the success of children. In 2014, the magazine was back at it again with another issue almost entirely devoted to fatherhood. "It's an interesting time in our cultural history," Granger noted, because there is now "a generation of young fathers that is taking an active, some would say obsessive interest in their families."[47] Writing in that issue, Mark Warren illustrated Granger's point. "Fatherhood is mostly defined by moments," Warren keenly observed, wondering if he was providing enough and the right kind of brief, fleeting snippets of time with his children. While Warren had considerable insight into what makes a good father, he did not consider himself a "natural" one, a thought that no doubt occurs to many if not most dads from time to time.[48]

Perhaps no other recent article in *Esquire*, or any other magazine for that matter, stated the value of contemporary fatherhood so clearly and compellingly as one written by Stephen Marche in 2014. In his "Manifesto of the New Fatherhood," Marche laid out nine principles that outlined the key themes of paternity today, encapsulating much of what has recently been written and said on the subject. As others had, Marche connected the problems stemming from widespread fatherlessness (currently affecting 25 percent of American families) with the significant roles dads now play, these two inverse conditions intrinsically (and perhaps oddly) intertwined.[49]

More than that, however, Marche perceived that the presence of an adult male in family life was still underestimated, that is, that we had yet to recognize the full worth of fatherhood. The new kind of fatherhood that had worked its way into the fabric of American society was "reshaping contemporary life," he argued, cutting across private and public arenas, political party lines, and all social divisions. Much had deservedly been made of the major social movements that had taken place in the country over the past half century—civil rights, the sexual revolution, greater equality for women in the workplace—but the less discussed transformation of fatherhood was arguably as important. No real heroes had been assigned to the new fatherhood movement, no historical canon had been created, and no cultural chaos had occurred, obscuring the true impact of its development. More unfair, the modern dad has been largely ridiculed in popular culture for challenging accepted notions of masculinity, this too eclipsing his contributions to American life. "Men, as fathers, are more crucial than anybody realized," Marche summed up, believing they were dramatically altering the economic, social, and political landscape of the nation.[50]

Esquire is not the only magazine to shed light on such weighty paternal deliberations. *GQ*, another prominent voice of the hedonistic lifestyle to be had by single men, also occasionally features interesting articles about fatherhood, as does *Men's Health*, whose pages are generally about fitness and wellness. The recognition of and respect to fatherhood paid by men's magazines is all too rare in the entertainment media, I believe, as it is a generally accurate reflection of the masculinity that is inherently embedded in being an American dad. Not just movies and television but women's magazines usually fall short in this regard, still clinging to the never true idea that fatherhood, like motherhood, is primarily a feminine domain.

For those who still maintain that fatherhood is a less-than-masculine pursuit, "dadchelor parties" serve as a resounding retort. Much like how Geoff Williams decided to host baby showers for "expectant dads" when he and his pals were not invited to the ones thrown for pregnant moms, some men are now manning up at parties catering specifically to soon-to-be fathers. Knowing that fun will be in limited supply after their respective babies arrive, men get together at these pre-delivery parties that are decidedly dude-centric. Golf is usually involved, not surprisingly, as is an extended session of drinking (with a designated driver or limo there to take the boys home, of course). Dean McDermott, the actor and husband of reality star Tori Spelling, included skeet shooting at his dadchelor party, an activity unlikely to be found at a typical baby shower. Moms appear to be less-than-enthusiastic supporters of these soirees (just 19 percent said they approved of them in a very unscientific poll on Facebook), but a certain kind of man will no doubt continue to declare his masculinity to his buddies via such events before having a child.[51]

Inevitably, perhaps, the "hipster dad" has also made his presence known in recent years. Although such fathers can be easily detected in capitals of cool like Austin, Texas, and Portland, Oregon, by their retro clothes and interesting facial hair, the hipster dad is arguably most at home in Brooklyn, New York. In fact, there is a Brooklyn-based magazine dedicated to this brand of young, urban father who views, as James Collins of the *New Yorker* put it, "locally sourced, artisanal children as the ultimate affectation." "We're trying to be fathers the way a cook nowadays chooses ingredients and pays attention and takes time," conceded one of the founders of *Kindling Quarterly*, which explores fatherhood through essays, interviews, editorials, art, and photography. While perhaps a bit over the top, the community of fathers who identify themselves with the image of the magazine is not just unapologetic about but deservedly proud of the domestic roles it has taken on. Most refreshing, this subculture of dads embraces a thoroughly positive orientation toward fatherhood, rejecting the standard trope that the enterprise is far more stressful than fun.[52] Also to his credit, the hipster dad, who is highly likely to hold some type of creative job, does not silo his work life from his role as parent. Parenting itself is a creative process, the publishers and readers of *Kindling Quarterly* would agree, an interesting perspective of fatherhood that is bound to gain greater traction in the years ahead.[53]

Hipster dads are, of course, only one of many branches currently growing on the big tree of American fatherhood. ("Punk dads" have also been observed.) The formation of various subcultures within American fatherhood over the past half century is one of its key strengths, a reflection of the pluralistic nature of the country itself. LGBT dads are another vital and expanding group who are broadening the definition of fatherhood and, in the process, raising its cultural profile and status. Just as the online community of straight dads is thriving via the blog universe, gay fathers are connecting with each other through various websites. A notable one is *The Handsome Father* (thehandsomefather. org), a national nonprofit organization designed to help gay fathers with everything from mentoring programs to adoption and surrogacy resources. "You can be your authentic self and you can still be a father," says Andy Miller, cofounder of *The Handsome Father*, who, along with his partner, Brian Stephens, adopted a son in 2006. Miller and Stephens gained a wealth of knowledge going through the adoption process and by being dads, the impetus for them to share that information with other gay men. Many gay men did not have positive role models for fatherhood, making a resource like *The Handsome Father* a particularly valuable one. Just one in five gay men is a parent (versus one in two lesbians), according to the Williams Institute at UCLA's School of Law, in part because of the lack of support given to this demographic. "Fatherhood has changed my world," Miller wrote on his blog in 2014, a sentiment most other dads would echo.[54]

Other gay fathers have presented their take on fatherhood and the interesting ways it changed their world. In his *Does This Baby Make Me Look Straight? Confessions of a Gay Dad*, Dan Bucatinsky humorously offered insight into the world of gay fatherhood, finding both much in common with and significant differences from the experiences of straight men. Like Miller and Stephens, Bucatinsky, a television writer and producer, and his partner adopted a child, giving them firsthand knowledge of the adventures of gay fatherhood and parenthood in general.[55] In his equally funny *The Kid: What Happened after My Boyfriend and I Decided to Get Pregnant* from a few years back, Dan Savage told the story of how he and his partner adopted their baby boy, not at all an easy process. *The Kid* was "a story about confronting homophobia, falling in love, getting older, and getting a little bit smarter," he wrote, but ultimately "a book about the very human desire to have a family."[56]

Lesbians have their fair share of compelling stories about how they started families. Interestingly, some lesbians report they identify more with the traditional role of a masculine, versus feminine, parent, giving rise to what has been termed the "lesbian dad." A good number of such women, whether in partnerships or as single parents, are even referring to themselves as "dad" or "daddy," not content with the gender-related associations that come with "mom" or "mommy." "It feels uncomfortable for some lesbians who are more male-identified to have their children call them 'mom' because this does not match their own gender identity, presentation, and the way they see their parental role," explained Abbie Goldberg, author of *Lesbian and Gay Parents and Their Children: Research on the Family Life Cycle*. Just like male heterosexual fathers, lesbian dads tend to be highly involved parents, this too explaining why the title seems to fit so well for some women with kids. "It is this cultural flux and blurring of gender roles that is opening space for all sorts of nontraditional parenting roles, including lesbian dads, to exist," the *Advocate* noted in reporting the phenomenon, with the concept of equal-shared parenting the common denominator.[57]

DADDY BRAIN

Underneath all the fragmentation or splintering of American fatherhood is the very simple fact that the presence of a dad in a family is a good thing. Disparate sources continue to make known the benefits of fatherhood for children, especially when dads are integrally involved in the lives of their young ones. In 2012, for example, Brigham Young University's School of Family Life found that dedicated fathers had a positive impact on kids' learning in school, while that same year the *Journal of Political Economy* published a study showing that actively engaged dads helped to build in children a general ethos of success. None of this was breaking news, of course, with previous research going back decades indicating much the same thing. Such findings were also to some so obvious that there was little point in reporting them or even conducting the studies. "When will we accept that fathers help their children with, well, everything?" Shawn Bean asked, claiming that many if not most dads were themselves perfectly aware of the ways they added to their kids' lives.[58]

While the positive effects of children upon fathers are less documented, there is abundant evidence that most dads (and moms) become more complete people through the process of parenting. This form of growth is almost always unexpected and far greater than anticipated, with fatherhood bringing out a side of oneself that one could not possibly know existed. "The profound implications of fatherhood fall fairly far afield of my previous human interactions," *American Spectator* contributing editor Shawn Macomber reflected on his daughter Ruth's first birthday, a fancy way of saying that his early parental experience was remarkable. There was no way for Macomber or any other new father to know that the wee hours of the morning could be so filled with anything but sleep, for example, the joys to be had sharing special moments far outweighing the subsequent fatigue. Part of the magic of fatherhood was the fragility of it, that the hazards of life made it all the more precious. "Could there be any greater blessing in life than to experience the transformational purity of a relationship that necessarily exists entirely in the moment?" he asked, the answer to that good question being an unequivocal no.[59]

As virtually every dad can tell you, many of the best moments taking place between a father and child involve some form of play. For decades now, researchers have shown there is much more to paternal playing than mere amusement. There is "a method to the madness" of fathers' boisterous playing style, many experts agree, crediting it with not only being really fun for kids but with such important things as building bravery. Landing in the ER is always a risk, of course, but this is much more of a concern for nervous moms observing the antics than dads instigating them. (Fathers are known to share a "no-need-to-tell-mommy-about-this" secret with their kids after an especially lively play session, establishing a powerful connection with a male role model.) "Dads push kids to do things that are frightening and exciting which helps them develop the ability to deal with unfamiliar situations," said Steven E. Rhoads, author of *Taking Sex Differences Seriously*, believing that the element of surprise and even flirting with danger were developmental positives. Many preschools in fact use play as their educational approach to effective learning, lending pedagogical support to something men seem to inherently know. Dads are simply better than moms at acting "childish" (in the best sense of the word), one could safely say, a characteristic children fully appreciate and benefit from.[60]

Study after study is also showing that the different respective parenting styles of men and women are not just culturally based but biologically as well. Just as there is a "mommy brain" programmed to coddle children, researchers have found, there appears to be a "daddy brain" designed to put their abilities to the test. Men "play an outsized role in challenging their kids and stretching their emotional and cognitive capabilities, preparing them for the big wide world," wrote Emily Anthes in *Scientific American Mind* after reviewing the growing body of research dedicated to understanding why fathers act the way they do. It was in the 1970s when most social scientists concluded that men were just as capable as women in taking care of their children (challenging John Bowlby's landmark 1958 paper "The Nature of the Child's Tie to His Mother" and the subsequent development of attachment theory). Over the next few decades, more attention was paid to the physiological changes of men as they became fathers—specifically the rise in the hormone prolactin (primarily associated with new mothers) and correlative drop in testosterone. More recently, however, research has shifted to how men are different from women in a biological sense than how they are alike when parenthood beckons. It is clear that men approach childcare from a recognizably male orientation that is at least as much rooted in biology as in social norms, making fatherhood quite literally masculine.[61]

Scientists have recently found, however, that men do share something with women in a biological sense: postpartum depression, or PPD. "Sad dads" is believed to be an increasingly common condition but one that is rarely discussed because it runs directly against the grain of the popular image of brand-new fathers gleefully passing out cigars to other men. Guys gung ho about becoming a father while their partners were pregnant are known to experience the "baby blues" in the first few days, weeks, or months after delivering, shaken by the nearly complete change in routine. As with new moms, brain chemistry is a contributing factor for paternal PPD, just as it is for "standard" depression. Paradoxically, perhaps, "type A" personalities are more likely to experience PPD, their emotional balance thrown off course by losing some control of situations. "I felt trapped and started spending longer hours at work because I didn't want to come home and be guilty about the way I was feeling," said one sufferer of the condition, describing himself as a "zombie going through the motions." One-quarter of men showed signs of depression when their baby was between the age of three and six months old, an article in the *Journal of the American Medical Association* reported, making male PPD a significant but largely overlooked health concern.[62]

The most cutting-edge biological research related to fatherhood, however, is clearly that associated with neuroscience. "When men morph into fathers, they experience a neural revival that benefits their children," Brian Mossop explained in *Scientific American Mind*, with both baby's and dad's brains forever altered in the days following birth. A biochemical bond is quickly established between fathers and their children, analogous to the one forged between mothers and their fetuses during pregnancy. Dads' brains are hardwired to respond to any threat to their infants' comfort and survival, for example, just one way oxytocin (the "love hormone") affects early paternal behavior. Fathers' and babies' brains function symbiotically, neuroscientists are finding, each party benefiting in some way from the other's cognitive influence. Men even grow new, additional neurons after becoming fathers, studies have shown, nature's way of establishing an emotional connection that will pay off dividends throughout the child's life.[63]

If the idea of some kind of cognitive symbiosis taking place is not amazing enough, a father's brain will alter its hormonal outputs and neural activity depending on his particular parenting responsibilities. Dads' brains can switch back and forth between a network geared toward social bonding and vigilance and one designed for planning and thinking, according to a 2014 study published in *Proceedings of the National Academy of Sciences*, changing its output based on the situation. Nurture is certainly important in parenting, but as in an increasing number of other activities, it is nature that researchers are discovering predisposes an individual toward certain behavior. Being a "good" parent is thus heavily determined by the brain's wiring, this research suggests, making us rethink much of what we have assumed about the practice of fatherhood.[64] Although fatherhood has been around as long as humans, we are clearly embarking on a new frontier of understanding it, with many exciting adventures no doubt looming for the future.

CONCLUSION

A cultural history of American fatherhood reveals important insights related to family life and gender identity—each a fundamental part of any society. Over the past half-century, dads in this country made great strides in advancing their role as parents, in the process helping to reshape our very social fabric. One of the primary goals of this book was to demonstrate that fathers matter (and matter quite a bit), something I believe is made abundantly clear throughout the story. That fathers are an instrumental, perhaps critical, component of the domestic sphere is a relatively new idea, historically speaking. Both anecdotal observations and hard research have shown that dads have a profound impact on the lives of their children, one that differs quite a bit from that of mothers. Some critics still fail to recognize this despite the findings of dozens of studies conducted over the last few decades. If the positive effects of an actively involved father are not obvious enough, the deleterious outcomes that often occur when one is absent should be perfectly evident. Fatherlessness is nothing short of a national tragedy, clearly illustrating the worth of a male parent in children's lives.

As a historian steeped in the typically conflict-oriented field of American studies, I have to confess that telling what I see as a happy story is refreshing. Much American history is about uncovering the darker sides of our nation's past, making this tale of what can be legitimately described as "male liberation" somewhat unusual. Beginning in the mid-1970s, men were able to throw themselves fully into a dimension of life that had been considered largely off-limits. Men eagerly seized this major opportunity as social and cultural norms regarding fatherhood relaxed, giving them access to an experience traditionally dominated by women. The new fatherhood, which ran roughly parallel with what became known as the "men's movement," was in some ways the inverse of second-wave feminism.[1] Equivalent but very different gains were made by men in their own struggle to earn equal rights and respect, a historical achievement that has gone largely ignored. Again, it may be farfetched to view men as a marginalized group within any context, but in light of this story, they could be considered as having been domestically disenfranchised prior to the nation's bicentennial. Of the handful of revolutionary social, technological, and scientific developments of the past half century, the transformation of fatherhood stands out for its influence in shaping the lives of two full generations of Americans. Today, men of all stripes have the chance to be the fathers they want to be, something simply not possible in the past, and children have the chance to be loved in a manner that also differs from yesterday.

Given this kind of gender empowerment, it is difficult to buy into the oft-mentioned "decline of men" theory. The patriarchal power of men has certainly diminished over the course of the last century and a half in the United States, but this has little to do with the real gains made in parenting. The deal, if there was one, was good for all members of society and the nation as a whole. Not only does the workplace operate much better as a more equal playing field, but family life has benefited from the greater contributions of dads. Men especially profited with this exchange of gender roles via their ability to express their personal identity as equal, or nearly equal, parents. Importantly, men were ultimately not required to give up any of their masculinity to achieve full parental status. In fact, a good case could be made that men advanced their level of "manhood" with the expansion of the meaning and practice of fatherhood, something critics have not fully appreciated.

The new kind of fatherhood that has flourished during the last forty years in this country was a difficult but, I believe, inevitable development. A strong emotional bond between father and child is very much biologically based, recent neuroscience has shown, meaning it is encoded into the wiring of our brains. It is not an exaggeration to say that the model of paternity that emerged in the last quarter of the twentieth century operated at a species level, a form of behavior that was consistent with our collective genetic makeup. Social and cultural norms caught up with biology, it could be said, the right interpretation of fatherhood in the right place at the right time. Men have always had strong attachments to their children, revisionist histories have demonstrated, but expressing them with a hefty dose of tenderness and sensitivity just did not fit the conventions of past times. Clearly defined gender roles provided a form of social stability, giving a bipolar view of family history that was heavily artificially constructed. Raising children was a lot grayer than the black-and-white universe it was portrayed as, although there is no doubt that the last few decades represent an exponential leap in men's ability to fully express themselves as parents.

While men now have the opportunity to father as they wish, significant challenges remain. First and foremost, being a parent is among the toughest jobs there are, as little compares with the responsibilities that come with taking care of another, dependent individual. Even in the best of circumstances, children are not easily managed creatures, I can safely tell you, with many aspects of parenting plainly beyond one's control. And as all fathers (and mothers) have learned, parenting fundamentally conflicts with pursuits of the self; it is difficult if not impossible to think and act as an individual while at the same time looking out for the best interests of a child. The aphorism that parenting is "all joy and no fun" has much truth to it, I believe, with an entirely different kind of pleasure to be enjoyed post- versus pre-child. As well, the search for balance that many parents have sought continues to be an elusive one, not surprising given the often contradictory relationship between oneself and one's family.

While the postwar dad was not as distant as he is usually remembered to be, the last half century brought forth changes that radically altered the nature of fatherhood. The new fatherhood was informed by the self-help movement of the 1970s, New Age thinking in the 1980s and 1990s, and our pervasive therapeutic culture, each of these instrumental in helping men get in touch with and express their feelings, including those regarding their children. Perhaps even more significant than the emergence of this more nurturing kind of dad was, again, the diversification of fatherhood. Many different sorts of dads appeared on the scene, each of them increasingly recognized for their ability to take care of a child versus their marital status, occupation or income level, sexual orientation, or lifestyle. Today fatherhood is a patchwork quilt of masculinity, the former defined more as a source of personal identity than prescribed social institution. Anyone doubting such might want to check out a few daddy blogs, where a cross section of men discuss any and every issue imaginable that is related to fatherhood. The Internet has played a key role in accelerating the diversity of fatherhood and helped position dads as a community of men with considerable cultural currency.

While it is relatively easy to reflect on the past of American fatherhood, predicting its future is more challenging. What happened yesterday is often not a good basis to forecast what will happen tomorrow, for one thing, and fatherhood is a subject steeped in the complexities of gender and family dynamics. Still, there are signs pointing the way to where fatherhood in America is likely heading over the next decade or so. The most critical issue is certainly fatherlessness, as what can fairly be described as an epidemic ravages underclass African American family life in this country. Attempts to reduce the number of absentee dads have been made for over a generation now, with the results less than encouraging. While considerable money has been invested in government-funded initiatives dedicated to promoting "responsible fatherhood," no one seems to know if the programs are working. "There is a lack of research that shows a definitive, causal link between participating in the program and changes in fathers' behavior and children's outcomes," reads a recent report from the Fatherhood Research and Practice Network, a five-year national project funded through the Department of Health and Human Services.[2]

In addition to these extensive public programs have been stepped-up legal efforts to force fathers to be more responsible should they decide not to do so voluntarily. Stronger laws have been passed to make noncustodial fathers pay child support, and it is now more difficult for deadbeat dads to receive welfare. Not much success can be directly tied to these measures as well, suggesting that a different tack should be taken. In their book *Doing the Best I Can: Fatherhood in the Inner City*, sociologists Kathryn Edin and Timothy J. Nelson argued that courts should award unwed fathers part-time custody of their kids, something rarely being done for this segment of the population. Such an effort might reconnect families, even if they are fragmented, precisely what happened after divorced middle- and upper middle-class dads with "cash, courage, and conviction" fought for custody rights in the 1970s. Positive steps like this one offer a much better chance of improving the situation than do harsher punitive measures.[3]

Fortunately, many men continue to see being a dad as "the role of a lifetime," as encouraging a sign as any that the future of fatherhood in the United States looks bright. Brad Pitt, one of the most famous men in the world, is in this fraternity, serving perhaps as a role model for others who look up to celebrities like him. Being a father makes Pitt "feel like the richest man alive," he recently said, adding that parenting is "the most beautiful thing you can experience." Married now to Angelina Jolie and the father of six, the superstar has slowed down his career in order to spend more time with his kids while they were still young, the same thing millions of ordinary Joes are doing.[4]

The fate of fatherhood in America depends in part on how men and women can balance their personal and professional lives. Paternity leave for new fathers is not a new issue, but there is currently more attention to it as more men try to figure out ways they can be both a great employee and a great dad. Both in its magazine and on its website, the *Atlantic* has recently taken a hard look at paternity leave, an example of the rising interest in what is a somewhat contentious battleground. (The issue has in fact been referred to as "the daddy wars," a reference to "the mommy wars" of decades past when women fought for maternity leave.) Some states require that companies grant men leave after their partner has a baby, while other firms voluntarily offer it, leaving the matter open for debate. Many sensibly believe that paternity leave is a good thing in that it offers men the opportunity to emotionally bond with their infants at a crucial time, not to mention that it gives moms a much-needed occasional break. If more men took up companies on their offer of leave, other men would as well, less afraid of the possible consequences of taking a couple of months away from work. The company perk also benefits working mothers, it should be said, as women would be more likely to take advantage of extended leave privileges should paternity leave become more of a standard practice among new fathers.[5]

How fatherhood evolves over the next decade and longer also has much to do with how dads are treated in popular culture and by society as a whole. Despite all the progress men have made as parents, they are still frequently belittled by the media and suffer from gender stereotyping. It is not unusual for dads to be cast as "overgrown children and second-class parents," according to Aaron Gouveia, host of the blog *The Daddy Files*. Setting the bar so low for men as parents does real damage, Gouveia believes, as some no doubt decide they should live up to such expectations. Fathers are caught between a rock and a hard place, he suggests, blamed for either working too much or spending too much time at home with the kids when they should be bringing more money into the household. And on television, in movies, and in advertising, it still is not unusual for fathers to be cast as buffoons, further spreading the untruth that men are just not up to the task of childcare.[6]

New media is more likely to portray fathers in an accurate light, however, something that bodes well for them as the Internet becomes an even greater presence in our lives. In the documentary series *Fatherhood*, for example, which could be seen on AOL.com in 2014, actor Hank Azaria naturally played himself—a middle-aged man who was ambivalent about having a first child. (Spoiler alert: he and his wife had one by the end of the series.) Social media is a bubbling cauldron of personal snippets related to fatherhood, with millions of dads or dads-to-be letting others know their innermost thoughts on the matter through text, photos, and videos. Facebook of course allows users to keep friends regularly informed of, well, whatever, and Instagram is a site to share one's life with the world through a series of pictures. Other popular social media sites also serve as fascinating communities of fatherhood. One recent remark on Pinterest: "Looking forward to fatherhood. A goal that should be on the mind of men. Made a vow between myself and God that I wouldn't be like my father but exceed the expectations of what it means to be a black father." Another from Twitter: "One of my proudest moments of Fatherhood so far . . . I convinced my near 2 year olds to watch 'Elf' instead of 'Frozen' tonight." If even one man can achieve such a thing, I believe the future of American fatherhood looks bright indeed.

NOTES

INTRODUCTION

1. Leonard Benson, *Fatherhood: A Sociological Perspective* (New York: Random House, 1968), 12.

2. David Blankenhorn, *Fatherless America: Confronting Our Most Urgent Social Problem* (New York: Basic Books, 1996), 1.

3. Ross D. Parke, *Fatherhood* (Cambridge: Harvard University Press, 1996), 13, 15; for more insight into the psychological and social aspects of fatherhood, see William Marsiglio, *Fatherhood: Contemporary Theory, Research, and Social Policy* (New York: Russell Sage Foundation, 1995); Wade C. Mackey, *The American Father: Biocultural and Developmental Aspects* (New York: Plenum Press, 1996); Nancy E. Dowd, *Redefining Fatherhood* (New York: New York University Press, 2000); Anna Gavanas, *Fatherhood Politics in the United States: Masculinity, Sexuality, Race, and Marriage* (Urbana: University of Illinois Press, 2004); and William Marsiglio and Kevin Roy, *Nurturing Dads: Social Initiatives for Contemporary Fatherhood* (New York: Russell Sage Foundation, 2012).

4. See E. Anthony Rotundo, *American Manhood: Transformations in Masculinity from the Revolution to the Modern Era* (New York: Basic Books, 1994), and Michael Kimmel, *Manhood in America: A Cultural History* (New York: Free Press, 1996), for authoritative histories of masculinity and manhood in the United States. For other interesting takes on the subject, see Kenneth Clatterbaugh, *Contemporary Perspectives on Masculinity: Men, Women, and Politics in Modern Society* (Boulder, CO: Westview Press, 1996); Guy Garcia, *The Decline of Men: How the American Male Is Getting Axed, Giving Up, and Flipping Off His Future* (New York: Harper, 2009); and Michael Kimmel,

Misframing Men: The Politics of Contemporary Masculinities (New Brunswick, NJ: Rutgers University Press, 2010). Important works in the expanding field of "masculinity studies" are R. W. Connell, *Masculinities* (Berkeley: University of California Press, 2005); Todd W. Reeser, *Masculinities in Theory: An Introduction* (Hoboken, NJ: Wiley-Blackwell, 2010); and Rachel Adams and David Savran, eds., *The Masculinity Studies Reader* (Hoboken, NJ: Wiley-Blackwell, 2012).

    5. Kathleen Gerson, *No Man's Land: Men's Changing Commitments to Family and Work* (New York: Basic Books, 1994), ix.

    6. Robert L. Griswold, *Fatherhood in America: A History* (New York: Basic Books, 1993), 16.

    7. Shawn Johansen, *Family Men: Middle Class Fatherhood in Industrializing America* (New York: Routledge, 2001).

    8. Stephen M. Frank, *Life with Father: Parenthood and Masculinity in the Nineteenth-Century American North* (Baltimore: Johns Hopkins University Press, 1998), 2.

    9. Ralph LaRossa, *The Modernization of Fatherhood: A Social and Political History* (Chicago: University of Chicago Press, 1997), 17.

    10. Griswold, *Fatherhood in America*, 93.

    11. LaRossa, *Modernization of Fatherhood*, 13.

    12. Griswold, *Fatherhood in America*, 143–44.

    13. Griswold, *Fatherhood in America*, 161–62.

    14. Ralph LaRossa, *Of War and Men: World War II in the Lives of Fathers and Their Families* (Chicago: University of Chicago Press, 2011), 2.

    15. Lawrence R. Samuel, *Pledging Allegiance: American Identity and the Bond Drive of World War II* (Washington, DC: Smithsonian Institution Press, 1997).

    16. Elaine Tyler May, *Homeward Bound: American Families in the Cold War Era* (New York: Basic Books, 1988).

    17. Griswold, *Fatherhood in America*, 186.

1. AMERICA'S NEWEST
ENDANGERED SPECIES

    1. John Leo, "Dominant Mothers Are Called Key to Hippies," *New York Times*, August 6, 1967, 78.

    2. George Gent, "TV: Poignant Study of Generation Gap," *New York Times*, August 13, 1969, 95.

    3. John Crosby, "Expectant Fathers Face Some Pregnant Questions," *Los Angeles Times*, January 7, 1968, D6.

4. Colman McCarthy, "American Fatherhood—Love at Distance?," *Boston Globe*, June 17, 1973, 3.

5. C. Christian Beels, "Whatever Happened to Father?," *New York Times*, August 25, 1974, SM220.

6. Marjorie R. Leonard, "When Fathers Drop Out," *New York Times*, April 20, 1969, SM81.

7. Leonard, "When Fathers Drop Out."

8. Carlfred B. Broderick, "Fathers," *Family Coordinator*, July 1977, 269–75. Even today, gender studies equates with women's studies at most universities.

9. Kenneth Gross, "Fatherhood," *Newsday*, November 10, 1970, 1A.

10. Bruce Voeller and James Walters, "Gay Fathers," *Family Coordinator*, April 1978, 149–57.

11. Voeller and Walters, "Gay Fathers."

12. Voeller and Walters, "Gay Fathers."

13. Brian Miller, "Gay Fathers and Their Children," *Family Coordinator*, October 1979, 544–51.

14. Enid Nemy, "Bachelor Fathers Who Are Planning to Adopt More Children," *New York Times*, November 12, 1973, 42.

15. Daniel D. Molinoff, "The Fathers: Conviction, Courage and Cash," *New York Times*, May 22, 1977, SM199.

16. Dennis K. Orthner, Terry Brown, and Dennis Ferguson, "Single-Parent Fatherhood: An Emerging Family Life Style," *Family Coordinator*, October 1976, 429–37.

17. Daniel D. Molinoff, "Father Knows Best," *New York Times*, June 24, 1975, 33.

18. Molinoff, "The Fathers: Conviction, Courage and Cash."

19. Molinoff, "The Fathers: Conviction, Courage and Cash."

20. Molinoff, "Father Knows Best."

21. Peter Anderson, "Custody Countdown," *Boston Globe*, November 16, 1973, 33.

22. Michael McFadden, *Bachelor Fatherhood: How to Raise and Enjoy Your Children as a Single Father* (New York: Walker, 1974).

23. Dolores Barclay, "The Rewards of Bachelor Fatherhood," *Los Angeles Times*, February 16, 1975, G20.

24. William Gildea, "The Joys and Trials of Parenthood When You're Male and Single," *Washington Post*, January 3, 1975, B1.

25. Molinoff, "Father Knows Best."

26. Robert Hanley, "Fathers' Group to Fight Custody Decisions," *New York Times*, March 7, 1977, 57.

27. Hanley, "Fathers' Group to Fight Custody Decisions."

28. Hanley, "Fathers' Group to Fight Custody Decisions."

29. Harriet Shapiro, "A Father with Custody of Two, Dr. Lee Salk Tells How to Help Children Cope with Divorce," *People Weekly*, June 19, 1978, 55.

30. Georgia Dullea, "Who Gets Custody of Children? Fathers Are Now Being Heeded," *New York Times*, October 14, 1975, RE44.

31. Sharon Johnson, "Divorced Fathers Organizing to Bolster Role in Children's Lives," *New York Times*, August 1, 1977, TR37.

32. Johnson, "Divorced Fathers Organizing."

33. Howard Crook, "Part-Time Fathers Struggle to Face a New Reality," *New York Times*, May 5, 1977, C1.

34. Warren Berry, "Fads," *Newsday*, June 13, 1978, 9A.

35. Judy Klemesrud, "Divorced Fathers' Weekend: Time to Reassert Love for Children," *New York Times*, June 2, 1969, F50.

36. Crook, "Part-Time Fathers."

37. Gail Brauner, "Parenthood after Divorce," *Health & Social Work*, May 1978, 331.

38. George Williams, "In Behalf of Fathers," *Health & Social Work*, May 1978, 331–34.

39. Harry Finkelstein Keshet and Kristine M. Rosenthal, "Fathering after Marital Separation," *Social Work*, January 1978, 11–18.

40. Crook, "Part-Time Fathers."

41. Georgia Dullea, "Divorced Fathers: Who Are Happiest?," *New York Times*, February 4, 1978, ST20.

42. Dullea, "Divorced Fathers."

43. Richard H. Gatley and David Koulack, *Single Fathers' Handbook: A Guide for Separated and Divorced Fathers* (New York: Anchor Doubleday, 1979).

44. Edith Atkin and Estelle Rubin, *Part-Time Father* (New York: Vanguard, 1975).

45. Jean Davies Okimoto, *My Mother Is Not Married to My Father* (New York: Putnam, 1979); Patricia Agre, *My Other-Mother, My Other-Father* (New York: Macmillan, 1979).

46. Judy Klemesrud, "Divorced Fathers' Weekend: Time to Reassert Love for Children," *New York Times*, June 2, 1969, F50.

47. Orthner, Brown, and Ferguson, "Single-Parent Fatherhood."

48. Helen A. Mendes, "Single Fatherhood," *Social Work*, July 1976, 308–12.

49. Keshet and Rosenthal, "Fathering after Marital Separation."

50. Klemesrud, "Divorced Fathers' Weekend."

51. Orthner, Brown, and Ferguson, "Single-Parent Fatherhood."

52. "Court Blocks an Abortion for Teen-Aged Student on Male Friend's Plea," *New York Times*, April 22, 1977, 23.

53. Arthur John Keeffe, "And Now, Fathers' Rights in Abortion Cases," *American Bar Association Journal*, December 1975, 1546–47.

54. Richard Flaste, "Fathers and Infants: Getting Close," *New York Times*, December 5, 1975, RE45.

55. Ross D. Parke, "The Father of the Child," *Sciences*, April 1979, 12–15.

56. Michael E. Lamb, ed., *The Role of the Father in Child Development* (Hoboken, NJ: Wiley, 1976); Marshall L. Hamilton, *Father's Influence on Children* (Chicago: Nelson-Hall, 1977).

57. Joseph W. Maxwell, "The Keeping Fathers of America," *Family Coordinator*, October 1976, 387.

58. Fitzhugh Dodson, *How to Father* (Los Angeles: Nash Publishing, 1974).

59. Henry Biller and Dennis Meredith, *Father Power* (New York: McKay, 1975); Sara D. Gilbert, *What's a Father For?* (New York: Warner, 1975).

60. Maureen Green, *Fathering* (New York: McGraw-Hill, 1976).

61. "Womens Way Salutes Fathers Day," *Philadelphia Tribune*, June 17, 1978, 23.

62. William Reynolds, *The American Father: A New Approach to Understanding Himself, His Woman, His Child* (New York: Paddington, 1978).

63. "State Hires Ex-F.B.I. Man to Hunt Missing Fathers," *New York Times*, January 8, 1973, 114.

64. Wolfgang Saxon, "Welfare Drive Seeks to Locate Absentee Fathers," *New York Times*, August 8, 1976, 42.

65. Jessica Benjamin, "Authority and the Family Revisited: or, A World without Fathers?," *New German Critique* (Winter 1978): 35.

66. Phyllis Chesler, "Sons and Fathers," *New York Times*, April 13, 1978, A23.

67. Bradley Soule, Kay Standley, and Stuart A. Copans, "Father Identity," *Psychiatry*, August 1, 1979, 255.

68. "Carter Proclaims Father's Day," *New York Times*, May 1, 1979, B8.

2. THE NEW FATHERHOOD

1. Anatole Broyard, "Bringing Back Father," *New York Times*, March 8, 1981, BR39.

2. "Superdads," *Futurist*, June 1985, 48.

3. Susan Muenchow and Jonathan Bloom-Feshbach, "The New Fatherhood," *Parents*, February 1982, 64–69.

4. Lynn Langway, "A New Kind of Life with Father," *Newsweek*, November 30, 1981, 93–94.

5. Paula Adams Hillard and J. Randolph Hillard, "The Expectant Father," *Parents*, April 1983, 80–82.

6. "Pop Psychology: What Makes a Good Father," *Changing Times*, June 1982, 58–60.

7. Harry Stein, "Feelings Will Out," *Esquire*, October 1981, 26–27.

8. Harry Stein, "A Man of Progeny," *Esquire*, April 1985, 37–38.

9. David Osborne, "Beyond the Cult of Fatherhood," *Ms.*, September 1985, 81–84.

10. Michael Lamb, "Will the Real 'New Father' Please Stand Up?," *Parents*, June 1987, 78, 80.

11. Lamb, "Will the Real 'New Father' Please Stand Up?"

12. Lamb, "Will the Real 'New Father' Please Stand Up?"

13. Lamb, "Will the Real 'New Father' Please Stand Up?"

14. Lamb, "Will the Real 'New Father' Please Stand Up?"

15. Russell Baker, "Fathering," *New York Times*, June 20, 1982, SM14.

16. "Pop Psychology: What Makes a Good Father."

17. Paula Adams Hillard and J. Randolph Hillard, "Fathers' Role in Childbirth," *Parents*, December 1983, 100–102.

18. Philip Taubman, "Doubts in the Delivery Room," *New York Times*, October 21, 1984, SM72.

19. Taubman, "Doubts in the Delivery Room."

20. J. T. Miller, "Fathers Who Deliver," *Parents*, June 1981, 63–66.

21. Miller, "Fathers Who Deliver."

22. Ronna Kabatznick, "Nurture/Nature," *Ms.*, August 1984, 76.

23. Robert B. McCall, "The Importance of Fathers," *Parents*, August 1980, 82.

24. "Pop Psychology: What Makes a Good Father."

25. Wray Herbert and Joel Greenberg, ". . . But Sex Roles Remain," *Science News*, September 10, 1983, 172.

26. Robert B. McCall, "Fulltime Father: Staying Home with Baby," *Parents*, February 1984, 88.

27. Wray Herbert and Joel Greenberg, "Fatherhood in Transition . . . ," *Science News*, September 10, 1983, 172.

28. Lynn Langway, "A Chance for Young Fathers," *Newsweek*, October 24, 1983, 118.

29. Brock Brower, "A Dad Diminished," *New York Times*, August 26, 1984, SM58.

30. Richard Taylor, "A Fulfillment," *New York Times*, March 29, 1987, SM62.

31. Carey Winfrey, "Fatherhood Postponed," *New York Times*, July 28, 1985, SM48.

32. Ron Hansen, "The Male Clock," *Esquire*, April 1985, 104–6.

33. Jerry Adler, "Second Thoughts," *Esquire*, October 1985, 202.

34. Hugh O'Neill, "Daddy Cool," *Parents*, July 1986, 74–75.

35. Lamb, "Will the Real 'New Father' Please Stand Up?"

36. Molly Haskell, "Lights . . . Camera . . . Daddy!," *Nation*, May 28, 1983, 673–74.

37. Peter W. Kaplan, "Dads Who Knew Best," *Esquire*, June 1986, 168.

38. Bill Cosby, *Fatherhood* (New York: Doubleday, 1986).

39. Lawrence R. Samuel, *The American Middle Class: A Cultural History* (New York: Routledge, 2013).

40. Gail Gregg, "Putting Kids First," *New York Times*, April 13, 1986, SM47.

41. Barbara Kantrowitz, "The Real 'Mr. Moms,'" *Newsweek*, March 31, 1986, 52.

42. Colin Leinster, "The Young Exec as Superdad," *Fortune*, April 25, 1988, 233–34.

43. "The Superdad Juggling Act," *U.S. News & World Report*, June 20, 1988, 67–70.

44. Evan Thomas, "The Reluctant Father," *Newsweek*, December 19, 1988, 64.

45. Jerrold Lee Shapiro, "The Expectant Father," *Psychology Today*, January 1987, 36–39, 42.

46. Shapiro, "Expectant Father."

47. Larry Samuel, *Rich: The Rise and Fall of American Wealth Culture* (New York: AMACOM, 2007).

48. Thomas, "Reluctant Father."

49. "Dads' Rights," *Newsweek*, May 23, 1988, 74; Michael Fumento, "The H Baby Incident," *National Review*, June 24, 1988, 32–33.

50. Pat Wingert, "And What of Deadbeat Dads?," *Newsweek*, December 19, 1988, 66.

51. Marjory Roberts, "The Benefits of Fatherhood," *Psychology Today*, March 1989, 76.

52. Bernice Weissbourd, "Dads' Big Role," *Parents*, July 1989, 158.

53. Roger M. Barkin, "The Changing Role of Fathers," *USA Today Magazine*, July 1989, 56–57.

54. Barkin, "Changing Role of Fathers."

55. Jean Marzollo, "Help Your Husband Be a Great Dad," *Parents*, September 1989, 98.

56. Karen Levine, "Are Dads Doing More?," *Parents*, June 1989, 73.

57. "Bringing Up Daddy," *Esquire*, November 1989, 116.

3. THE DADDYTRACK

1. Marcus Mabry, "On Madison Avenue, Daddy Sells Best," *Newsweek*, November 12, 1990, 54.

2. Katherine Karlsrud and Dodi Schultz, "Helping Dads Help Out," *Parents*, May 1990, 200.

3. Erik Larson, "The New Father," *Parents*, June 1991, 90–94.

4. Marshall Karp, "66 Things Your Father Never Taught You," *Parents*, June 1992, 107–10.

5. Lisa Schroepfer, "Dad: New & Improved," *American Health*, June 1991, 64–69.

6. A. A. Brott, "Not All Men Are Sly Foxes," *Newsweek*, June 1, 1992, 14.

7. David S. Machlowitz, "TV Dads and Me," *Parents*, June 1990, 225.

8. Elayne Rapping, "Make Room for Daddy," *Progressive*, November 1993, 34–38.

9. Frank Pittman, "Fathers & Sons," *Psychology Today*, September/October 1993, 52–54.

10. Fred Barnes, "Quantity Time," *New Republic*, July 12, 1993, 42.

11. Benjamin Stein, "What a Good Dad Knows," *Washingtonian Magazine*, June 1997, 41–44.

12. Sean Elder, "Dabbling Dads," *New York Times*, June 11, 1995, SM30.

13. Richard Louv, "How Fathers Feel . . . ," *Parents*, December 1993, 226–34.

14. Robert J. Samuelson, "Why Men Need Family Values," *Newsweek*, April 8, 1996, 43.

15. Louv, "How Fathers Feel . . ."

16. David Popenoe, "Parental Androgyny," *Society*, September/October 1993, 5–11.

17. "Clarifying the Meaning of Fatherhood," *USA Today Magazine*, December 1993, 7–8.

18. Sheldon H. Cherry, "Sharing the Pregnancy Experience," *Parents*, July 1991, 101.

19. Fay Stevenson-Smith and Dena K. Salmon, "Dads in the Labor Room," *Parents*, January 1993, 101.

20. Ruth Pennebaker, "The Perfect Pregnant Father," *Parents*, August 1994, 55–56.

21. Jerrold Lee Shapiro, "Letting Dads Be Dads," *Parents*, June 1994, 165–68.

22. Jerry Adler, "Wait Till Daddy Gets Home!," *Good Housekeeping*, January 1997, 80–83.

23. Shapiro, "Letting Dads Be Dads."

24. Nancy Seid and Annis Golden, "Becoming a Dad: How Men 'Nest' Differently from Women," *Parents*, February 1997, 77–78.

25. Katherine J. Sweetman, "Paternal Separation Anxiety," *Harvard Business Review*, July/August 1995, 14.

26. Ellis Cose, "The Year of the Father," *Newsweek*, October 31, 1994, 61.

27. Richard Louv, "Al Gore on Fatherhood," *Parents*, February 1995, 45.

28. Louv, "Al Gore on Fatherhood."

29. Joseph P. Shapiro and Joannie M. Schrof, "Honor Thy Children," *U.S. News & World Report*, February 27, 1995, 38.

30. Elizabeth Schoenfeld, "Our Foundering Fathers," *Policy Review*, January 1996, 18.

31. David Blankenhorn, "Pay, Papa, Pay," *National Review*, April 3, 1995, 34–38.

32. David Popenoe, *Life Without Father* (New York: Free Press, 1996).

33. "Leading the Fatherhood Brigade," *Policy Review*, January 1996, 19.

34. "Leading the Fatherhood Brigade."

35. Wade F. Horn, "You've Come a Long Way, Daddy," *Policy Review*, July–August 1997, 24–30.

36. Horn, "You've Come a Long Way, Daddy."

37. Ann Hulbert, "Angels in the Infield," *New Republic*, November 18, 1996, 46.

38. Paul Roberts, "Fathers' Time," *Psychology Today*, May/June 1996, 49–55, 81.

39. Jerry Adler, "Building a Better Dad," *Newsweek*, June 17, 1996, 58.

40. Adler, "Building a Better Dad."

41. Marc Myers, "The Invisible Dad," *Parents*, June 1996, 97–98.

42. Sheldon Himelfarb, "Laws of the Jungle Gym," *Parents*, November 1994, 245.

43. "Make Room for Daddy," *Redbook*, June 1996, 98–103.

44. Wade F. Horn, "Keeping Fathers Involved," *Better Homes and Gardens*, August 1998, 102, 104.

45. Christine Winquist Nord, DeeAnn Brimhall, and Jerry West, "Dads' Involvement in Their Kids' Schools," *Education Digest*, March 1998, 29.

46. Peter Rubin, "Family Man," *New Republic*, April 27, 1998, 12–13.

47. "Dream Dads," *Parents*, June 1998, 123–24.

48. Joanna Powell, "Interview: Paul Reiser," *Good Housekeeping*, September 1997, 32.

49. "Fathers and Sons," *People*, November 16, 1998, 124.

50. "The Grateful Dad," *People*, June 28, 1999, 60.

51. Judith Davidoff, "The Fatherhood Industry," *Progressive*, November 1999, 28.

52. Cal Fussman, "Jake LaMotta," *Esquire*, June 1999, 118.

53. Mary Beth Grover, "Daddy Stress," *Forbes*, September 1999, 202–8.

54. Keith H. Hammonds, "The Daddy Trap," *Business Week*, September 21, 1998, 56–64.

55. Davidoff, "The Fatherhood Industry."

56. Davidoff, "The Fatherhood Industry."

57. Davidoff, "The Fatherhood Industry."

58. Davidoff, "The Fatherhood Industry."

59. Frederic Golden and Annie Murphy Paul, "Making Over Mom and Dad," *Psychology Today*, May/June 1999, 36–40, 73–75.

60. Margaret Carlson, "Does He or Doesn't He?," *Time*, April 27, 1998, 22.

4. THE ROLE OF A LIFETIME

1. Michael Snider, "She Calls Me 'Dadadada,'" *Maclean's*, June 20, 2005, 50.

2. Amy Dickinson, "Daddy's Big Moment," *Time*, June 19, 2000, 146.

3. Cathy Young, "The Sadness of the American Father," *American Spectator*, June 2000, 40.

4. Susan McClelland, "Why Dads Matter," *Maclean's*, June 18, 2001, 34–35.

5. Benedict Carey, "The Secret Life of a Stay-at-Home Dad," *Redbook*, March 2000, 104.

6. Carey, "Secret Life of a Stay-at-Home Dad."

7. Susan Horsburgh, "Daddy Day Care," *People*, June 23, 2003, 79–82.

8. Patrick McCormick, "Make Room for Daddy," *U.S. Catholic*, February 2002, 42.

9. McCormick, "Make Room for Daddy."

10. "Today's Dads: Same Old Parenting Trap," *Business Week*, October 14, 2002, 167.

11. Douglas Carlton Abrams, "Father Nature: The Making of a Modern Dad," *Psychology Today*, March/April 2002, 38.

12. Dana Scarton, "Postpartum Depression Strikes New Dads as Well as Moms," *U.S. News & World Report*, September 29, 2008, 83.

13. Andrew Pyper, "The Ticking Daddy Clock," *Maclean's*, April 29, 2002, 52.

14. Valerie Frankel, "The Truth about Fatherhood," *Parenting*, May 2003, 164.

15. Frankel, "Truth about Fatherhood."

16. Frankel, "Truth about Fatherhood."

17. Geoff Williams, "A Dad's Guide to Bonding with Baby," *Baby Talk*, June/July 2003, 71.

18. Williams, "Dad's Guide to Bonding with Baby."

19. Charlie Gillis, "Reporting for Diaper Drill, Sir!," *Maclean's*, July 31, 2006, 46–47.

20. Ayelet Waldman, "My Husband, the Perfect Mom," *Parenting*, November 2004, 81–82.

21. Fred Leebron, "I Am Man, Hear Me Bleat," *Parenting*, April 2004, 197–98.

22. "Don't End Up Fathering by Default," *USA Today Magazine*, October 2006, 16.

23. Michael Douglas, "The Role of a Lifetime," *Newsweek*, September 17, 2007, 82.

24. "Kevin Costner," *Good Housekeeping*, June 2007, 54.

25. Bill Templeman, "I'm Dad, not Granddad," *Maclean's*, April 5, 2004, 54.

26. Jennifer Wolff, "The Mortal Man," *Best Life*, June 2007, 95.

27. Marc Parent, "How to Be an Even Better Dad," *Best Life*, May/June 2005, 50.

28. Hugh O'Neill, "Embrace the Uncertainty," *Best Life*, March 2007, 82–83.

29. Sam Grobart, "The Newborn Ultimatum," *Best Life*, November 2008, 98.

30. Christopher Healy, "Macho, Macho Dad," *Parenting*, November 2007, 176–77.

31. Erik Strand, "Out of Touch," *Psychology Today*, January/February 2004, 24.

32. David Russell, "A Modern Infant Armada," *Maclean's*, August 16, 2004, 54.

33. Geoff Williams, "A Baby Shower Just for Fathers," *Baby Talk*, February 2006, 73.

34. Geoff Williams, "Our Guy Tries to 'Have It All,'" *Baby Talk*, March 2006, 67–69.

35. Eve Heyn, "The Daddy Track," *Parenting*, September 2003, 155–56.

36. Heyn, "Daddy Track."

37. Heyn, "Daddy Track."

38. Michele Orecklin, "Stress and the Superdad," *Time*, August 23, 2004, 38–39.

39. Geoff Williams, "Study-Hall Slacker," *Baby Talk*, March 2005, 77–78.

40. Brian Braiker, "Just Don't Call Me Mr. Mom," *Newsweek*, October 8, 2007, 52–55.

41. Hugh O'Neill, "The Mission of a Lifetime," *Best Life*, June 2007, 95.

42. Michael Finkel, *Blindsided by a Diaper* (New York: Three Rivers Press, 2007).

43. Andrew Postman, "Loving Another," *Parenting*, October 2002, 213–14.

44. Douglas Carlton Abrams, "The Daddy Dividend," *Psychology Today*, March/April 2002, 40.

45. Aviva Patz, "Help Fathers Be Dads," *Redbook*, June 2007, 212.

46. Jason Feifer, "8 Lessons All Dads Should Teach," *Men's Health*, October 2009, 68.

47. Glen Freyer, "Married to the Mob," *Parenting*, September 2008, 145.

48. Kenneth Whyte, "Stephan Poulter, Clinical Psychologist, Author of *The Father Factor* and Dad to a 12-Year-Old Girl Talks to Kenneth Whyte," *Maclean's*, May 1, 2006, 17–18.

49. Joshua Alston, "O Father, Where Art Thou," *Newsweek*, May 19, 2008, 45.

50. Alston, "O Father, Where Art Thou."

51. Geoff Williams, "Boob-Tube Blues," *Baby Talk*, March 2007, 76–77.

52. Williams, "Boob-Tube Blues."

53. "Confessions: Moms Dish on Dads," *Parenting*, June 2008, 129–30.

54. Jason Daley, "Pop Goes the Weasels," *Best Life*, October 2008, 44.

55. Josh Dean, "Paul Bettany," *Best Life*, March 2006, 80–81.

56. Rick Newman, "Single Dad, Efficient Parent," *Parenting*, March 2007, 116–17.

57. David Kushner, "Daddy Day," *Parenting*, May 2008, 135–36.

58. "Dads Domesticated by Encouragement," *USA Today Magazine*, October 2008, 8–9.

59. Nancy Gibbs, "Dads Are Dudes," *Time*, June 29, 2009, 56.

60. Emily Bloch, "The Daddy Difference," *Parenting*, June 2007, 80–84.

61. Fernanda Moore, "Inside the Mind of a Dad," *Parenting*, June 2006, 84–90.

62. Lorraine Ali, "The 'New Dad'? Give Me a Break," *Newsweek*, October 8, 2007, 54–55.

63. Shawn Bean, "Manny Knows Best," *Baby Talk*, October 2009, 70.

64. Michael Lewis, *Home Game* (New York: W. W. Norton, 2009).

5. MANNY KNOWS BEST

1. Shawn Bean, "Gary Poppins," *Parenting School Years*, July 2012, 44.

2. Barack Obama, "Being the Father I Never Had," *People*, June 20, 2011, 70–74.

3. Obama, "Being the Father I Never Had."

4. Julia Marsh, "Fatherhood, Not Marriage, Is Focus of Obama Family Policies," *Christian Science Monitor*, August 10, 2010, 7.

5. Marsh, "Fatherhood, Not Marriage."

6. J. B. Wogan, "More Money for Fatherhood Programs, But No New Law," *Tampa Bay Times*, July 20, 2012.

7. See www.fatherhood.gov for more information.

8. Samuel Goldsmith, "One-Third of Children in Our City Are Growing Up without a Father," *New York Daily News*, October 11, 2010, 14.

9. David Hirsch, "The Fatherhood Doctrine," *Chicago Tribune*, June 16, 2013, 1:20.

10. Pamela Paul, "Are Fathers Necessary?," *Atlantic*, July–August 2010, 62–63.

11. Brian Caulfield, "The End of Men?," *Human Life Review* (Winter 2010): 64–70.

12. Gary Drevitch, "Pop Psychology," *Psychology Today*, June 2014, 40–41.

13. Shawn Bean, "My Gritty, Grimy, Filthy To-Do List," *Parenting*, June 2011, 44.

14. Paul Scott, "The New American Dad," *Parents*, July 2010, 84–91.

15. Hannah Seligson, "Neither Moms nor Imbeciles," *New York Times*, February 24, 2013, BU1.

16. Shawn Bean, "The Modern Dad, Redefined," *Parenting*, April 2011, 60.

17. Joanne Latimer, "Ex-wives Rail about Phony Facebook Dads," *Maclean's*, June 20, 2011, 84.

18. Lawrence R. Samuel, *Death, American Style: A Cultural History of Dying in America* (Lanham, MD: Rowman & Littlefield, 2013).

19. Mark Warren, "My Father's Last Words," *Esquire*, June/July 2012, 172–94.

20. Stephen Marche, "Why Fatherhood Matters," *Esquire*, June/July 2013, 82–88.

21. Marche, "Why Fatherhood Matters."

22. Kim Painter, "New Dads Can Be a Cautious Lot," *USA Today*, June 14, 2010, D4.

23. V. Jeffrey Evans, "How Do Children Affect the Health and Well-Being of Fathers?," *Fathering*, Spring 2014, 117.

24. Tia L. Zeno and Robert M. Kaplan, "Social, Financial, Emotional and Biological Effects on Fathering," *Fathering* (Spring 2014): 174.

25. Sharon Jayson, "'The Other Half' of Parenting Story Is Told," *USA Today*, June 13, 2013, D2.

26. Brad Harrington, Fred Van Deusen, and Jamie Ladge, "The New Dad: Exploring Fatherhood within a Career Context," Boston College Center for Work and Family, June 2010.

27. Harrington, Van Deusen, and Ladge, "The New Dad: Exploring Fatherhood."

28. Brad Harrington, Fred Van Deusen, and Beth Humberd, "The New Dad: Caring, Committed and Conflicted," Boston College Center for Work and Family, 2011.

29. Brad Harrington, Fred Van Deusen, and Iyar Mazar, "The New Dad: Right at Home," Boston College Center for Work and Family, 2012.

30. Harrington, Van Deusen, and Mazar, "The New Dad: Right at Home."

31. Catherine Richards Solomon, "'I Feel Like a Rock Star,'" *Fathering* (Winter 2014): 52.

32. Solomon, "'I Feel Like a Rock Star.'"

33. Brad Harrington, Fred Van Deusen, and Jennifer Sabatini Fraone, "The New Dad: A Work (and Life) in Progress," Boston College Center for Work and Family, 2013.

34. Harrington, Van Deusen, and Fraone, "The New Dad: A Work (and Life) in Progress."

35. Marche, "Why Fatherhood Matters."

36. Aaron Traister, "A Real Guy Takes on TV Dads," *Redbook*, October 2012. See Donald Unger, *Men Can: The Changing Image and Reality of Fatherhood in America* (Philadelphia: Temple University Press, 2010), for an excellent examination of positive and negative depictions of fathers in pop culture.

37. James Poniewozik, "Daddy Issues," *Time*, June 18, 2012, 60.

38. Shawn Bean, "Parentism," *Parenting School Years*, July 2012, 42.

39. "Don't Underestimate Dad," *Chicago Tribune*, June 17, 2012, 23.

40. Jill Herzig, "Do-It-All Dads," *Redbook*, June 2012, 10.

41. "Hot Dads with Babies," *Redbook*, June 2012, 26.

42. Jenna McCarthy, "Superdad Is Driving Me Nuts," *Babytalk*, March 2011, 68.

43. Jessica Baumgardner, "The New Daddy Guilt," *Redbook*, February 2013, 112.

44. Shawn Bean, "Baby Daddy on Board," *Babytalk*, March 2011, 70.

45. David Granger, "What a Man Does," *Esquire*, June/July 2012, 28.

46. David Curcurito, "Free as a Bird," *Esquire*, June/July 2012, 165.

47. David Granger, "FAQs with the Editor," *Esquire*, June/July 2014, 22.

48. Mark Warren, "Fatherhood for Men," *Esquire*, June/July 2014, 96–97.

49. Stephen Marche, "Manifesto of the New Fatherhood," *Esquire*, June/July 2014, 118–21.

50. Marche, "Manifesto of the New Fatherhood."

51. Janene Mascarella, "Say 'I Dude,'" *Parenting*, May 2013, 13.

52. Christopher Maag, "Eschewing the Stress of Fatherhood in Favor of the Fun," *New York Times*, February 11, 2013, A17.

53. James Collins, "Daddy-O," *New Yorker*, June 3, 2013, 20–21.

54. Heidi Stevens, "Helping Gay Men Navigate the Path to Fatherhood," *Chicago Tribune*, May 25, 2014, 6.2.

55. Dan Bucatinsky, *Does This Baby Make Me Look Straight? Confessions of a Gay Dad* (New York: Touchstone, 2012).

56. Dan Savage, *The Kid: What Happened after My Boyfriend and I Decided to Get Pregnant* (New York: Plume, 2000).

57. Abby Dorsey, "The New Lesbian Dad," *Advocate*, April/May 2013, 34.

58. Shawn Bean, "The Duh Report," *Babytalk*, March 2013, 48.

59. Shawn Macomber, "Year One," *American Spectator*, April 2014, 64.

60. Joe Kita, "The Daddy Factor," *Parents*, June 2013, 132–36.

61. Emily Anthes, "Family Guy," *Scientific American Mind*, May/June 2010, 46–53.

62. Margery D. Rosen, "Sad Dads," *Parents*, April 2013, 122.

63. Brian Mossop, "How Dads Develop," *Scientific American Mind*, July/August 2011, 31–37.

64. Michael Brooks, "In the Brain of the Father," *New Statesman*, July 18, 2014, 13.

CONCLUSION

1. For more on the men's movement, see Michael Messner, *Politics of Masculinities: Men in Movements* (Lanham, MD: Rowman & Littlefield, 1997), and Michael Schwalbe, *Unlocking the Iron Cage: The Men's Movement, Gender Politics, and American Culture* (New York: Oxford University Press, 1996). Robert Bly, *Iron John: A Book about Men* (Reading, MA: Addison-Wesley, 1990), is considered more or less the manifesto of the movement.

2. For more information, visit www.frpn.org.

3. Mark Stricherz, "Baby Daddies," *First Things*, November 2014.

4. Tessa Berenson, "I Want to Spend More Time with My Kids," *Time.com*, October 3, 2014.

5. For one such article, see Liza Mundy, "Daddy Track: The Case for Paternity Leave," *Atlantic*, January/February 2014, www.theatlantic.com/magazine/archive/2014/01/the-daddy-track/355746/.

6. Aaron Gouveia, "Emma Watson Is Right—Don't Take Potshots at Fathers," *Time.com*, November 13, 2014.

SELECTED BIBLIOGRAPHY

Adams, Rachel, and David Savran, eds. *The Masculinity Studies Reader*. Hoboken, NJ: Wiley-Blackwell, 2012.

Agre, Patricia. *My Other-Mother, My Other-Father*. New York: Macmillan, 1979.

Apple, Sam. *American Parent: My Strange and Surprising Adventures in Modern Babyland*. New York: Ballantine, 2009.

Atkin, Edith, and Estelle Rubin. *Part-Time Father*. New York: Vanguard, 1975.

Barkin, Roger M. *The Father's Guide: Raising a Healthy Child*. Golden, CO: Fulcrum Publishing, 1988.

Benson, Leonard. *Fatherhood: A Sociological Perspective*. New York: Random House, 1968.

Biller, Henry, and Dennis Meredith. *Father Power*. New York: McKay, 1975.

Biller, Henry B., and Robert J. Trotter. *The Father Factor: What You Need to Know to Make a Difference*. New York: Gallery Books, 1994.

Blankenhorn, David. *Fatherless America: Confronting Our Most Urgent Social Problem*. New York: Basic Books, 1996.

Bly, Robert. *Iron John: A Book about Men*. Reading, MA: Addison-Wesley, 1990.

Boswell, John, and Ron Barrett. *How to Dad*. New York: Dell, 1990.

Brott, Armin. *Fathering Your School-Age Child: A Dad's Guide to the Wonder Years*. New York: Abbeville Press, 2007.

———. *Fathering Your Toddler: A Dad's Guide to the Second and Third Years*. New York: Abbeville Press, 2005.

———. *The New Father: A Dad's Guide to the First Year*. New York: Abbeville Press, 2004.

———. *The Single Father: A Dad's Guide to Parenting without a Partner*. New York: Abbeville Press, 1999.

Brott, Armin, and Jennifer Ash. *The Expectant Father: Facts, Tips, and Advice for Dads-to-Be*. New York: Abbeville Press, 2010.

Bucatinsky, Dan. *Does This Baby Make Me Look Straight? Confessions of a Gay Dad*. New York: Touchstone, 2012.

Canfield, Ken. *The Seven Secrets of Effective Fathers*. Carroll Stream, IL: Tyndale House, 1992.

Carnoy, Martin, and David Carnoy. *Fathers of a Certain Age: The Joys and Problems of Middle-Aged Fatherhood*. London: Faber & Faber, 1995.

Clatterbaugh, Kenneth. *Contemporary Perspectives on Masculinity: Men, Women, and Politics in Modern Society*. Boulder, CO: Westview Press, 1996.

Coates, Ta-Nehisi. *The Beautiful Struggle: A Father, Two Cons, and an Unlikely Road to Manhood*. New York: Spiegel & Grau, 2009.

Connell, R. W. *Masculinities*. Berkeley: University of California Press, 2005.

Cosby, Bill. *Fatherhood*. New York: Doubleday, 1986.

Dodson, Fitzhugh. *How to Father*. Los Angeles: Nash Publishing, 1974.

Dowd, Nancy E. *Redefining Fatherhood*. New York: New York University Press, 2000.

Edin, Kathryn, and Timothy J. Nelson. *Doing the Best I Can: Fatherhood in the Inner City*. Berkeley: University of California Press, 2013.

Finkel, Michael. *Blindsided by a Diaper*. New York: Three Rivers Press, 2007.

Frank, Stephen M. *Life with Father: Parenthood and Masculinity in the Nineteenth-Century American North*. Baltimore: Johns Hopkins University Press, 1998.

Garcia, Guy. *The Decline of Men: How the American Male Is Getting Axed, Giving Up, and Flipping Off His Future*. New York: Harper, 2009.

Gatley, Richard H., and David Koulack. *Single Fathers' Handbook: A Guide for Separated and Divorced Fathers*. New York: Anchor Doubleday, 1979.

Gavanas, Anna. *Fatherhood Politics in the United States: Masculinity, Sexuality, Race, and Marriage*. Urbana: University of Illinois Press, 2004.

Gerson, Kathleen. *No Man's Land: Men's Changing Commitments to Family and Work*. New York: Basic Books, 1994.

Gilbert, Sara D. *What's a Father For?* New York: Warner, 1975.

Goldberg, Abbie E. *Lesbian and Gay Parents and Their Children: Research on the Family Life Cycle*. New York: American Psychological Association, 2010.

Green, Maureen. *Fathering*. New York: McGraw-Hill, 1976.

Greenberg, Martin. *The Birth of a Father*. New York: Continuum, 1985.

Greene, Bob. *Good Morning, Merry Sunshine: A Father's Journal of His Child's First Year*. New York: Atheneum, 1984.

Griswold, Robert L. *Fatherhood in America: A History*. New York: Basic Books, 1993.

Hamilton, Marshall L. *Father's Influence on Children*. Chicago: Nelson-Hall, 1977.

Harrington, Brad, Fred Van Deusen, and Beth Humberd. "The New Dad: Caring, Committed and Conflicted." Boston College Center for Work and Family, 2011.

Harrington, Brad, Fred Van Deusen, and Jamie Ladge. "The New Dad: Exploring Fatherhood within a Career Context." Boston College Center for Work and Family, 2010.

Harrington, Brad, Fred Van Deusen, and Iyar Mazar. "The New Dad: Right at Home." Boston College Center for Work and Family, 2012.

Harrington, Brad, Fred Van Deusen, and Jennifer Sabatini Fraone. "The New Dad: A Work (and Life) in Progress." Boston College Center for Work and Family, 2013.

Hass, Aaron. *The Gift of Fatherhood: How Men's Lives are Transformed by Their Children*. New York: Touchstone, 1994.

Heinowitz, Jack. *Pregnant Fathers: Becoming the Father You Want to Be*. Kansas City, MO: Andrews McMeel, 1997.

Hill, David. *Dad to Dad: Parenting Like a Pro*. Elk Grove, IL: American Academy of Pediatrics, 2012.

Johansen, Shawn. *Family Men: Middle Class Fatherhood in Industrializing America*. New York: Routledge, 2001.

Kimmel, Michael. *Manhood in America: A Cultural History*. New York: Free Press, 1996.

———. *Misframing Men: The Politics of Contemporary Masculinities*. New Brunswick, NJ: Rutgers University Press, 2010.

Lamb, Michael E., ed. *The Role of the Father in Child Development*. Hoboken, NJ: Wiley, 1976.

LaRossa, Ralph. *The Modernization of Fatherhood: A Social and Political History*. Chicago: University of Chicago Press, 1997.

———. *Of War and Men: World War II in the Lives of Fathers and Their Families*. Chicago: University of Chicago Press, 2011.

Levinson, Daniel J. *The Seasons of a Man's Life*. New York: Ballantine, 1979.

Lewis, Michael. *Home Game*. New York: W. W. Norton, 2009.

Lewis, Paul. *The Five Key Habits of Smart Dads: The Secrets of Fast-Track Fathering*. Grand Rapids, MI: Zondervan, 1994.

Lynn, David B. *The Father: His Role in Child Development*. Belmont, CA: Wadsworth Publishing, 1974.

Mackey, Wade C. *The American Father: Biocultural and Developmental Aspects*. New York: Plenum Press, 1996.

Marsiglio, William, ed. *Fatherhood: Contemporary Theory, Research, and Social Policy*. New York: Russell Sage Foundation, 1995.

Marsiglio, William, and Kevin Roy. *Nurturing Dads: Social Initiatives for Contemporary Fatherhood*. New York: Russell Sage Foundation, 2012.

May, Elaine Tyler. *Homeward Bound: American Families in the Cold War Era*. New York: Basic Books, 1988.

McCall, Robert B. *Infants*. New York: Vintage Books, 1980.

McFadden, Michael. *Bachelor Fatherhood: How to Raise and Enjoy Your Children as a Single Father*. New York: Walker, 1974.

Messner, Michael. *Politics of Masculinities: Men in Movements*. Lanham, MD: Rowman & Littlefield, 1997.

Okimoto, Jean Davies. *My Mother Is Not Married to My Father*. New York: Putnam, 1979.

Parke, Ross D. *Fatherhood*. Cambridge, MA: Harvard University Press, 1996.

Parke, Ross, and Armin Brott. *Throwaway Dads: The Myths and Barriers That Keep Men from Being the Fathers They Want to Be*. New York: Houghton Mifflin, 1999.

Pemeranz, Virginia E., and Dodi Schultz. *The First Five Years*. New York: St. Martin's Press, 1991.

Pittman, Frank. *Man Enough: Fathers, Sons, and the Search for Masculinity*. New York: Putnam Adult, 1993.

Pleck, Elizabeth H., and Joseph H. Pleck, *The American Man*. New York: Prentice-Hall, 1980.

Pleck, Joseph H. *The Myth of Masculinity*. Boston: MIT Press, 1981.

Pleck, Joseph, and Jack Sawyer, eds. *Men and Masculinity*. New York: Prentice-Hall, 1974.

Popenoe, David. *Life without Father*. New York: Free Press, 1996.

Poulter, Stephan. *The Father Factor: How Your Father's Legacy Impacts Your Career*. Amherst, NY: Prometheus, 2006.

Raeburn, Paul. *Do Fathers Matter? What Science Is Telling Us about the Parent We've Overlooked*. New York: Scientific American/Farrar, Straus & Giroux, 2014.

Reeser, Todd W. *Masculinities in Theory: An Introduction*. Hoboken, NJ: Wiley-Blackwell, 2010.

Reiser, Paul. *Babyhood*. New York: William Morrow, 1997.

Reynolds, William. *The American Father: A New Approach to Understanding Himself, His Woman, His Child*. New York: Paddington, 1978.

Rhoads, Steven E. *Taking Sex Differences Seriously*. New York: Encounter Books, 2005.

Ross, Carol. *Pop: A Celebration of Black Fatherhood*. New York: Stewart, Tabori & Chang, 2007.

Rotundo, E. Anthony. *American Manhood: Transformations in Masculinity from the Revolution to the Modern Era*. New York: Basic Books, 1994.

Salk, Dr. Lee. *What Every Child Wants His Parents to Know*. New York: David McKay, 1972.

Samuel, Larry. *Rich: The Rise and Fall of American Wealth Culture*. New York: AMACOM, 2007.

Samuel, Lawrence R. *The American Middle Class: A Cultural History*. New York: Routledge, 2013.

———. *Death, American Style: A Cultural History of Dying in America*. Lanham, MD: Rowman & Littlefield, 2013.

———. *Pledging Allegiance: American Identity and the Bond Drive of World War II*. Washington, DC: Smithsonian Institution Press, 1997.

Savage, Dan. *The Kid: What Happened after My Boyfriend and I Decided to Get Pregnant*. New York: Plume, 2000.

Schwalbe, Michael. *Unlocking the Iron Cage: The Men's Movement, Gender Politics, and American Culture*. New York: Oxford University Press, 1996.

Shapiro, Jerrold Lee. *When Men Are Pregnant*. Atascadero, CA: Impact Publishers, 1987.

Spangler, Doug. *Fatherhood: An Owner's Manual: For Fathers of Children from Birth to Age Five*. Richmond, CA: Fabus, 1994.

Unger, Donald. *Men Can: The Changing Image and Reality of Fatherhood in America*. Philadelphia: Temple University Press, 2010.

Vassel, Rachel. *Daughters of Men: Portraits of African-American Women and Their Fathers*. New York: Amistad, 2007.

INDEX

ABOUT THE AUTHOR

Lawrence R. Samuel holds a PhD in American studies from the University of Minnesota and was a Smithsonian Institution Fellow. He writes the "Psychology Yesterday" blog for *Psychology Today* and is the author of many books, including *Sexidemic: A Cultural History of Sex in America* (Rowman & Littlefield, 2013) and *Death, American Style: A Cultural History of Dying in America* (Rowman & Littlefield, 2013).